Lockh

C-141 Starlifter

BOB ARCHER

KEY
Books

HISTORIC MILITARY AIRCRAFT SERIES, VOLUME 9

Front cover image: One of the first C-141Bs for the 63rd Military Airlift Wing (MAW), 66-0128 is overflying its home base, Norton Air Force Base (AFB), with 25 A models on the flight line. (USAF)

Back Cover image: Former Tennessee Air National Guard (ANG) C-141C 66-0157 with a "For Sale" sign added to the nose before the aircraft flew to AMARC (Aircraft Maintenance and Regeneration Center) on May 3, 2004. (Doug Slowiak)

Contents page image: Seen during December 1987, Tennessee ANG C-141B 64-0622 is painted in the European One scheme, which would appear to be very effective overflying parts of the US. (Don Spering)

Acknowledgements
The author wishes to thank Mike Novack for his highly detailed C141Heaven web site, and also Woodrow "Woodie" Hall's C-141 Squadrons site. Additionally, British Aviation Review and the AMARC Experience website also supplied valuable details. Jeffery P Rhodes at Lockheed was a great help with individual aircraft histories. Former Starlifter air and ground crews provided many fascinating crumbs of knowledge, notably Gary Baker and John Vadas. Several friends freely contributed information and images, especially Paul Bennett, Paul and Phil Cossey, Steve Hill, Phil Kovaric, Kirk and Paul Minert, Mark Pestana, Doug Remington, and Doug Slowiak. Surprisingly, very little has been written about the Starlifter, with the few publications that are available not adequately catering for the enthusiast market. This book is intended to redress this inconsistency.

Published by Key Books
An imprint of Key Publishing Ltd
PO Box 100
Stamford
Lincs PE19 1XQ

www.keypublishing.com

ISBN 978 1 80282 043 0

Typeset by SJmagic DESIGN SERVICES, India.

Contents

Introduction

The Starlifter was in constant use by the US military from October 1964 until the last was retired on May 5, 2006. Almost 42 years of service was a significant achievement and testament to a design that solved the issue of large loads transported over intercontinental distances, rapidly. Lockheed clearly understood the combination of a high wing, for ground clearance, and a corresponding lower fuselage floor that enabled vehicles to load directly, enhancing turn-around time. As deliveries increased, so the Starlifter assumed the mantle of strategic airlift, and, within a short time, there was a C-141 airborne at every minute of every day. During five decades of service, the type achieved 10,611,720 flight hours, and landed on all seven continents.

Lockheed applied the slogan "C-141 Starlifter – promoting world peace and security, one flight at a time" to their first jet military aircraft. While this may seem cheesy, it nevertheless adequately sums up the role of the aircraft, which subsequently flew so many humanitarian missions. On August 23, 1963, President John F Kennedy proclaimed it was a "great moment for our nation" when he unveiled the initial Lockheed C-141 Starlifter by remote control from the White House. By ceremoniously turning a gold key in the nation's capital, he instigated the virtual rollout of the aircraft some 620 miles away. President Kennedy ushered the first steps of the new jet-powered airlifter into service, and set in motion the versatile C-141, which helped establish a benchmark in airlift operations for the second half of the twentieth century.

A bare metal C-141B outside the Warner Robins ALC during major overhaul. The scaffolding around the tail is testament to the high degree of attention paid to Planned Depot Maintenance. (Warner Robins ALC)

Chapter 1

In the Beginning

The Air Force ordered 284 C-141A models, with the manufacturer constructing one more to be retained as a demonstrator for the anticipated civilian market. Having earlier established a major production facility at Marietta to build the C-130 Hercules, Lockheed quite naturally chose the site, known as Air Force Plant 6 (AFP6), for the C-141. AFP6 was a government-owned installation, operated by Lockheed. Following the first Starlifter rollout, Lockheed averaged one aircraft completed every five days or so, ensuring the Air Force was able to effectively plan the introduction to its six operational strategic airlift units.

The fleet was ordered between 1961 and 1967. The first was 61-2775, which was retained by Lockheed and not officially delivered to the Air Force until December 12, 1969. The other four from fiscal year (FY) 1961 were also retained for a limited period, along with the first three from FY1963. The 100th Starlifter was handed over on April 22, 1966, while only one year later the figure was 226. The final aircraft was 67-0166, which was flown from Marietta to Tinker AFB, Oklahoma, on February 28, 1968, bringing Starlifter production to an end.

63rd MAW C-141A 64-0634 parked at Dayton, Ohio, in July 1970, while supporting the Thunderbirds team. (PMC)

Test and Evaluation

Understandably, the theoretical capabilities of any weapons system needed to be fully and rigorously evaluated by competent test personnel, to ensure it entirely matched the requirement in reality. Even a seemingly uncomplicated airlift aircraft such as the Starlifter needed such an assessment. The first eight aircraft, serials 61-2775 to -2779 and 63-8075 to -8077, were subjected to a demanding test and evaluation program, organized by Air Force Systems Command (AFSC). This was performed by test crews, primarily at Edwards AFB, California, but also at other AFSC facilities. General flight characteristics preceded investigation of loading and delivery techniques. The first three FY1961 aircraft, plus 63-8075 and 63-8076, were all designated as JC-141As during 1964, signifying temporary test. All had reverted to their normal designation by 1965. The latter aircraft was with the Aeronautical Systems Division (ASD) at Wright-Patterson AFB, Ohio, by December 1964 to determine airflow in various flight regimes. These were concluded within a year, enabling the aircraft to join the 436th Military Airlift Wing (MAW).

Left: Nose markings of *Petunia* C-141A 63-8075, seen here when performing a 2,500-hour test and evaluation staged between June 15, 1964, and May 16, 1965, at Edwards AFB. (via John Vadas)

Below: The sixth Starlifter built, 63-8075, was delivered to the Air Force Flight Test Center (AFFTC) at Edwards AFB on June 2, 1964. Despite the application of Military Air Transport Service (MATS) markings, the aircraft displays the Air Force Systems Command (AFSC) emblem on the nose. (AFFTC)

NC-141A 61-2776 wearing the basic Military Air Transport Service (MATS) color scheme of the period, but with Air Force Materiel Command (AFMC) lettering and insignia. Seen here overflying the desert area near Edwards AFB. (USAF)

C-141A 63-8075 was involved in a 2,500-hour Category II Systems Evaluation Test Program to generate a large number of sorties. This began on June 15, 1964, by the Air Force Flight Test Center (AFFTC) at Edwards AFB, with daily flights of more than 12 hours duration taking place for several months. The aircraft was the first to surpass 3,500 flight hours, and later 25,000, well ahead of any other Starlifter.

Four of the test aircraft were transferred to operational units when their period of evaluation duty was completed, while the other four, serials 61-2775, -2776, -2777 and -2779, were retained by AFSC. They relocated to ASD between 1967 and mid-1971, and were gradually redesignated as NC-141As, beginning in late 1970, as permanently assigned to test and development work.

First MATS Aircraft

The Military Air Transport Service (MATS) initiated their training program when 63-8078, named *Spirit of Oklahoma*, was handed over to the 1741st Air Transport Squadron (ATS), 1707th Air Transport Wing (ATW) at Tinker AFB on October 16, 1964. Nine more followed in quick succession to enable the first aircrew conversion course to begin. Initially, these were experienced personnel who had previously flown the Boeing C-135 Stratolifter, although a small number were from the Douglas C-124 Globemaster community. The first cadre graduating was streamlined into becoming instructors at Tinker, or joined 44th ATS, 1501st ATW at Travis AFB, California. Those assigned to Travis finalized preparations for the new airlifter to begin operations. The 44th was selected to initiate C-141 operations, as the unit had been equipped with the C-135B, and therefore personnel were familiar with turbo fan engines. Both aircraft types were powered by the Pratt & Whitney TF-33, although an enhanced version was fitted to the C-141 offering 12 percent more thrust.

The first Lockheed C-141A Starlifter delivery to the 44th ATS took place on April 23, 1965. The aircraft was 63-8088, named *The Golden Bear*, which was accepted during a ceremony attended by General Howell M Estes II, the legendary and visionary commander of the MATS. Sixteen C-141As had been delivered to Travis by September 3, 1965, when 64-0628 joined the squadron. By this time, Tinker had received 15 Starlifters and was conducting regular conversion courses.

Above: With the name *The Golden Bear* prominently displayed on the nose, C-141B 63-8088 is seen taxiing at Buckley Air National Guard Base (ANGB), Colorado, in February 1983. (John A Sheets)

Left: Throughout its entire operational career, 63-8088 carried the name *The Golden Bear*. (PMC)

Below: During Lead The Force (LTF) evaluation, 60th MAW C-141A 63-8088 made many trips to Vietnam, as seen here at Tan Son Nhut AB in April 1968. Despite being comparatively new, the aircraft is already showing signs of extensive use. Adjacent to the name *The Golden Bear* is the red LTF emblem. (Bob Burgess)

While MATS was supplanting their C-135s with the new C-141, the AFFTC was utilizing Starlifters in an enhanced flying program, named Lead the Force (LTF). This involved six dedicated aircraft achieving a very high sortie rate to identify any deficiencies. The aircraft involved were 63-8075, 63-8078, 63-8079, 63-8080, 63-8081 and 63-8088. LTF officially commenced on June 1, 1965, and produced 2,535 flight hours in just 11 months, with aircraft planned to fly eight hours a day, through until 1968. The unusually large number of flight hours and frequent inspections were designed to reveal any problems, such as corrosion, which might result from extended usage. Four aircraft were dedicated to extensive daily flying, completing short and long-distance sorties. The other pair flew more than twice the number of landings than other operational Starlifters to evaluate landing gear, spoilers, and flaps usage. Two were from the 1501st, while the other four were 1707th aircraft. At the completion of the LTF program, they resumed normal Military Aircraft Command (MAC) flight schedules. Lockheed supported the program from July 15, 1966, until March 5, 1968. Understandably, the high flight hour aircraft were periodically inspected to ensure that the LTF program did not produce any adverse effects on certain structural components and continued long after some of the aircraft had been reassigned to other units.

MATS Expands

C-141As were eventually delivered to seven MATS/MAC Wings. Apart from the 1501st and the 1707th ATWs already mentioned, the 1607th and 1608th ATWs, at Dover AFB, Delaware, and Charleston AFB, South Carolina, respectively, transitioned. The 1608th received 64-0624, while the 1607th accepted 64-0630 on the same day to initiate MATS Atlantic fleet operations. They were flown the short distance from Marietta on August 13, 1965 – with official acceptance into squadron service taking place on August 14 and 18, respectively. The third of the Atlantic Wings was the 438th MAW at McGuire AFB, New Jersey, whose first new aircraft, 66-7947, was delivered on August 8, 1967. Completing the units was

The first MATS Starlifter sortie to Europe was by 1607th Air Transport Wing (ATW) C-141A 64-0634 during October 1965. The aircraft was barely two weeks old when it departed Dover AFB for a six-day orientation visit. (Jack Friell)

the 62nd MAW at McChord AFB, Washington, which accepted 65-0277 and -0278 on August 5, 1966, and the 63rd MAW at Norton AFB, California, which took delivery of 66-0149 on January 6, 1967.

MATS conducted the initial Starlifter European orientation mission to evaluate the new aircraft at several major airlift bases. C-141A 64-0634, which was fourth to be delivered to the 1607th ATW, arriving on October 1, 1965, embarked upon visits to Chateauroux-Deols AB, France, Torrejón AB, Spain, Rhein Main AB, West Germany, and RAF Mildenhall, UK. This was between October 15 and 20, 1965, and enabled personnel at these facilities to appraise the new equipment. Earlier, in June 1965, 1501st ATW C-141A 63-8090 had participated at the Paris Air Show, although this was organized by Lockheed, rather than the Air Force. Two years later, 436th MAW 66-0174 was at the Paris Air Show.

Generally speaking, the three bases located in the US Pacific coastal region served Asian routes, while the trio of Starlifter bases adjacent to the Atlantic Ocean concentrated on those to Europe, Africa, and the Middle East.

Left: The first delivery to 1608th ATW was 64-0624, named *City of Charleston South Carolina*. Subsequently, 64-0610 became *City of Charleston II* by April 1986. (PMC)

Below: Statically displayed only eight weeks after delivery, 436th MAW C-141A 66-0174 is at Le Bourget for the Paris Air Show in late May 1967. Note the Paris park code 200 on the nose. (Steve Williams)

First Color Schemes

The first aircraft, 61-2775, was completed in natural metal finish, and marked with the insignia of MATS, consisting of a dark blue tail stripe outlined in yellow. The yellow service logo was applied to the rear fuselage, while the legend Military Air Transport Service was presented above the main undercarriage wheel well covers. The only additional marking was the application of the AFSC emblem on port side of the nose and AFFTC emblem on the starboard. The first eight aircraft all had the MATS markings, as well as those of AFSC. The majority of pre-service tests were performed by both AFFTC and the ASD. Having completed operational test and evaluation, half of the test fleet were transferred to operational units, with Wing unit insignia replacing the markings of the test organizations.

C-141A

USAF C-141As very quickly became regular visitors to all the usual MAC air bases worldwide. The majority of sorties flown from the western US airlift hubs were across the Pacific Ocean to South East Asia (SEA). To expedite the delivery of cargoes, a system called "stage" was introduced, whereby one crew flew the aircraft to a specific destination where their duty period finished. They would then go into crew rest, while the aircraft would be refueled, and prepared for the next leg of the journey. A fresh crew would then depart to the final destination. All too frequently crews from one unit would be flying an aircraft from another.

Above: 62nd MAW C-141A 65-9410 has a stylized map of Washington State and the name *Tacoma* on it. Note the 62nd MAW legend applied to the main wheel well, which was only a feature during the early period of operations. Seen here at Richmond, Australia, in June 1967. (Ben Dannecker)

Right: 62nd MAW C-141A 66-0165 taxiing at Sydney, Australia, in April 1969. Note the gray radome. (David Carter)

Experience with the Starlifter soon proved the investment was invaluable. However, equally quickly, the shortcomings of the payload became apparent, with the potential for a modification program, which for a comparatively modest investment, could provide a fuselage stretch to enable more cargo and/or passengers to be transported. This lengthening could be achieved with the existing powerplants, and without any other major modifications. Furthermore, the installation of an in-flight refueling system could be incorporated, thereby increasing range significantly. Lockheed issued a proposal to the USAF, which, after consideration, issued a contract. The C-141B was about to enhance Starlifter operations appreciably.

MAC Formed

MATS was replaced by Military Airlift Command (MAC) on January 1, 1966, enabling the new organization to efficiently control operations. MATS had been a Service, manned by personnel from both the Air Force and Navy, whereas the new organization was solely staffed by the former.

C-141A 64-0612 of the 437th MAW was a prolific visitor to Mildenhall, UK, gaining cult status, with the serial being written as graffiti on numerous non-aviation places (road signs, toilet doors, walls, railway carriages and a host of other places). This notoriety began as a joke and continued for many years. (Bob Archer)

A few years after conversion to C-141B standard and a repaint in European One, 64-0612 has 437th MAW on the nose but no other external unit details. Seen at Mildenhall in May 1987. (Bob Archer)

The infamous 64-0612 served with the 97th Air Mobility Wing (AMW) in a training role, before retirement to AMARC on February 1, 2000, as the 82nd example to be stored. (Bob Archer)

Air Transport Squadrons/Wings were redesignated as Military Airlift Squadrons/Wings. Furthermore, C-141 units with four-digit identities were renumbered, with the 1501st, 1607th, 1608th and 1611th (at McGuire, but which had yet to acquire C-141s), and 1707th becoming the 60th, 436th, 437th, 438th, and 443rd MAWs, respectively. The primary reason for the change of four-digit identifiers was that they were Major Command provisional units by the USAF due to MATS being a Department of Defense Unified Command. Under the USAF lineage system, they did not possess a permanent ancestry, and were therefore discontinued upon inactivation.

Following a visit to the southern hemisphere in December 1977, 63rd MAW C-141A 64-0614 was decorated with Day-Glo orange kangaroos. (PMC)

Above left: **Close-up of the additional "zaps" on C-141A 64-0614. (PMC)**

Above right: **Santa's sleigh being pulled by three kangaroos applied to the fuselage of C-141A 64-0614 during December 1977. (PMC)**

MATS had established set routes resupplying USAF bases, as well as those of the other Department of Defense Services. MAC retained these, but was directed to organize its own activities, with the new Starlifter at the forefront of airlift activities.

Civilian Proposal

Lockheed believed there was a civilian market for the C-141. During June 1963, a joint enquiry from Deutsche Lufthansa and the West German Air Force was made to Lockheed about acquiring C-141s. Further civilian interest was shown by Slick Airways in April 1964 for four aircraft, and, one month

Lockheed had their latest hardware on display during a sales drive at the 3rd International Air Forum held in Chicago during May 1966. In this extremely atmospheric image, the L-300 is prominently displayed alongside L-100 N1130E, and 60th MAW C-141A 64-0615. (Doug Slowiak)

The sole L-300, which was flown by NASA for much of its career, seen in September 1983. (Carl E Porter)

later, by Flying Tiger Airlines for eight, both of which issued contracts. However, all of these enquiries were conditional upon the Starlifter having an extended fuselage. As no such version was forthcoming initially, all withdrew interest.

Nevertheless, the 110th aircraft on the line was produced as the Lockheed L-300, with the civilian registration N4141A. The aircraft, painted white overall, with red markings, flew for the first time on May 4, 1966. The L-300 was shown to potential customers in many overseas countries, as well as the home market. Sadly, there were no buyers, and, after 704 flight hours, the aircraft was withdrawn on July 3, 1968.

At the end of 1970s, the National Aeronautics and Space Administration (NASA) was looking for a four-engined jet transport aircraft to mount the large astronomical telescope for the Gerard P. Kuiper Airborne Observatory. Successful negotiations and an upgrade were carried out before the aircraft joined NASA on February 3, 1972, becoming N714NA. The aircraft was flown to NAS Moffett Field, California, to join the Ames Research Center. This aircraft flew missions to various worldwide locations to perform high altitude sorties with the telescope, before being placed in storage at Moffett Field. The registration expired on April 24, 2013, and was put up for sale on August 10, 2018, but failed to meet the reserve price. Currently, it is stored externally at Moffett Field.

Chapter 2
Vietnam Support

T he war in Vietnam created an enormous demand for airlift, with the new C-141 increasingly assuming a greater burden of the resupply effort. The first flight by the type to the combat zone was on August 5, 1965, when a 1501st ATW aircraft delivered 50,000lb (22,679kg) of cargo to Tan Son Nhut Air Base in South Vietnam.

The standard routing for C-141As to South Vietnam was via Hickam AFB, Hawaii, Wake Island, Guam, and possibly Clark AB, Philippines, or Kadena AB, Okinawa/Yokota AB, Japan. From there, it was a short hop into South Vietnam. The C-141As departed the combat zone as soon as the aircraft were unloaded because of restricted space limitations. Tail winds on the return journey often enabled some of these refueling stops to be bypassed. Another regular routing was via McChord AFB, Washington, and Elmendorf AFB, Alaska. All operational Wings were involved. The drain upon regular MAC Starlifter squadrons resulted in the C-124s being retained by the reserves well into the 1970s. The Globemasters also supported the Vietnam campaign, as well as replacing many C-141 sorties to European destinations.

Starlifter sorties to Vietnam frequently routed to destinations such as Bien Hoa, Cam Ranh Bay, Da Nang, Pleiku, or Tan Son Nhut before returning home, involving a flight time of between 37 to 40 hours. A second route across the Pacific Ocean was from Travis to Wake Island, Clark, and into Vietnam, before returning home via Yokota. Occasionally, with the aid of a strong tailwind, the C-141 could fly direct to Travis. This routing could encompass 35 to 37 flight hours. Interestingly, the much slower C-124 would take 80 to 90 flight hours for the same journey. Whereas the Starlifter crew would be away from home for about one week, those flying the C-124 would take double that time.

Pilot Gary Baker has details from his logbook showing routes, flying times, and distances, which are an average as winds varied the times significantly. For example, his logbook flying time shows 4,800 miles between Yokota to Travis, which varied from 9.4hrs to 11.0hrs, depending upon the help from the prevailing jet stream:

Westbound
Travis to Hickam 5.7 hours (2,760 nautical miles); Hickam to Wake 5.4 hours (2,250 nm); Travis to Wake Island 9.4 hours (4,500 nm); Wake to Anderson AB, Guam 3.4 hours (1,460 nm); Wake to Kadena 5.6 hours (2,680 nm); Wake to Clark 6.5 hours (2,900 nm); Wake to Tan Son Nhut AB 8.8 hours (4,150 nm); Anderson to Clark 3.6 hours (1,500 nm); Clark to Saigon 2.5 hours (1,000 nm); Clark to Da Nang 2.4 hours (1,000 nm); Clark to Cam Ranh Bay 2.0 hours (1,000 nm); Clark to Bangkok IAP, Thailand 3.4 hours (1,450 nm)

Eastbound
Clark to Kadena 2.6 hours (1,050 nm); Clark to Yokota 3.8 hours (1,950 nm); Anderson to Yokota 4.0 hours (1,600 nm); Cam Ranh Bay to Yokota 5.0 hours (2,000 nm), Da Nang to Yokota 4.7 hours (2,140 nm); Kadena to Yokota 2.4 hours (1,050); Yokota to Hickam 7.6 hours (3,680); Yokota to Travis 10.4 hours (4,800 nm); Hickam to Travis 4.8 hours (2,760 nm) – Note the difference on this route between eastbound and westbound time, was often due to tail winds.

Indeed, a 437th MAW C-141A flew from Yokota AB nonstop to Charleston AFB in 14hrs and 10mins. Piloted by Lieutenant Colonel Ken Waggoner, the fairly new jet, with no cargo, planned for Elmendorf

436th MAW C-141A 65-0266 taxiing at an air base in Thailand in 1966. (Bob Archer collection)

AFB, then Scott AFB, but with optimum flight levels, and amazing supporting winds, it flew on to home station, landing with just 1,500lb of fuel. The wing commander was unimpressed, but Waggoner rightly earned an Air Medal!

Navigating the long distances between the islands was a very precise responsibility. Starlifter crews during the 1960s and 1970s included a navigator, who plotted their course using all available ground-based navigational aids. These were located at the air bases on islands across the ocean using Automatic Direction Finder, TACtical Air Navigation, and VHF Omni-Directional Range systems. Additionally, the US Coast Guard vessel *Ocean Station November* assisted with an accurate fix, if necessary, when the vessel was at sea. Furthermore, Baker also explained that if the conditions were right, the ADF could pick up a radio station such as KNBR in San Francisco, even from as far away as 2,000 miles. If there were troops aboard returning from Vietnam, the radio station would be relayed over the cargo hold speaker system, which enabled the boys to enjoy a little bit of the good old USA – apparently, they all loved this gesture!

The seemingly insatiable requirement for airlift to SEA continued throughout the remainder of the 1960s and into the 1970s. The Vietnamization Program, whereby many close-air-support assets and missions were transferred to the Republic of Vietnam, did little to stem the flow of cargo, although US personnel numbers were reduced.

For many years, senior government figures in Washington DC effectively managed the war, and prolonged the campaign significantly. This resulted in the flow of weapons, materials and personnel carrying on until early in 1973. The *Linebacker* offensive in December 1972 and into 1973 finally brought the North Vietnamese to the Paris Peace Accord. Apart from a fudged agreement whereby the US could vacate South Vietnam, the talks settled the plight of several hundred personnel who had been captured and imprisoned in North Vietnam.

Operation *Homecoming*

Repatriating US prisoners of the Vietnam War, mostly from captivity in the North, was performed under Operation *Homecoming*. US Secretary of State Henry Kissinger, acting on behalf of President Richard Nixon, negotiated the release after extensive discussions. Gia Lam Airport, in the eastern suburbs of Hanoi, was to be the departure airfield. The 22nd Air Force was tasked to provide C-141As to fly ex-POWs from Hanoi, with 15 Starlifters selected as the primary aircraft, and a further three as "unassigned" back up. Of the primaries, six each were to be provided by the 60th and 62nd MAWs, while three were from the 63rd MAW. All had a large red cross applied to the tail. Understandably, the aircraft chosen were the most reliable, and were especially prepared for their important mission, with airliner style seating, and comfort stations installed. These were as follows:

- 60th MAW 65-0236, 65-0238, 65-0259, 65-0280, 65-9398, 66-7944 primary, plus 65-0230 unassigned
- 62nd MAW 64-0641, 65-0232, 65-0243, 65-0258, 66-0161, 67-0031 all primary
- 63rd MAW 66-0177, 67-0001, 67-0007 primary, plus 66-0156, 66-7949 unassigned

The C-141s were flown to Clark AB, which was just 2hrs and 30mins flight time away from Hanoi. With plans in place, the first US aircraft to arrive was a USAF C-130E, reported by a crew member to possibly be 70-1274 of the 61st TAS, 314th Tactical Airlift Wing (TAW) from Little Rock AFB, Arkansas. The 776th TAS, 374th TAW from Ching Chuan Kang, Taiwan, administered the C-130

Left: 62nd MAW C-141A 66-0161 flew one Gia Lam and four Clark AB to the US sorties during Operation *Homecoming*. Released POW USAF Lt Col Daniel James Doughty walks from the Starlifter to the awaiting bus. (USAF)

Below: 65-0258 was one of six 62nd MAW C-141As dedicated to Operation *Homecoming* to repatriate former POWs from Hanoi. Seen here at McChord AFB on March 10, 1973. (Doug Remington)

aspect, with some of their aircraft also landing at Gia Lam. The Hercules ferried a small medical team, as well as a number of personnel of the 1st Mobile Communications Group. The latter established a link with the incoming C-141A, as well as higher headquarters in the South. On this and each subsequent occasion, a spare Starlifter was airborne off the coast of Da Nang to be available as a replacement, in the event one of the tasked aircraft developed technical issues.

The first three C-141As to land at Gia Lam were 66-0177, followed by 65-0243, and lastly 65-0236, which all did so on February 12, 1973. A total of 116 US Air Force, Navy and Marine Corps personnel were flown out on these Starlifters. The aircraft departed Hanoi between 1230hrs and 1445hrs local time for the short flight to Clark. Starlifter aircrew reported that on each flight, a huge cheer from the former captives erupted as the aircraft lifted off the Gia Lam runway. A further cheer filled the fuselage, as the pilot announced over the intercom that aircraft had cleared into international airspace. At Clark, the ex-POWs were given a medical, before being processed ready for their return to the US. Eight more batches of former POWs were repatriated through Gia Lam before the final group departed on March 29. The departure details were:

- February 12: 66-0177, 65-0243, 65-0236 with 116 passengers
- February 18: 64-0641 with 20
- March 4: 66-0177, 66-7944, 65-0243 with 111
- March 5: 66-0161 with 34
- March 14: 67-0007, 64-0641, 66-7944 with 108
- March 16: 65-0280 with 32
- March 27: 67-0001 with 32
- March 28: 67-0007, 67-0031 with 50
- March 29: 65-0280, 65-0238 with 67

Of the fifteen Starlifters allocated to the mission, eleven are known to have landed in North Vietnam. Apart from the flights from Gia Lam to Clark, there were 36 C-141A sorties from the Philippines to the US. These were carried out between February 13 and April 1, 1973.

As the first aircraft to fly out former POWs, 66-0177 was nicknamed *Hanoi Taxi* by the repatriated personnel. A flat panel above the flight engineers' station was inscribed with the nickname. Many of the repatriated personnel signed their names and added the period they were in captivity. Understandably, the aircraft gained notoriety, and thanks to the strenuous efforts of Technical Sergeants Dave Dillon, Jeff Wittman, and Henry Harlow at Wright-Patterson, they began a process to save the aircraft. Eventually, a plaque was affixed internally, and a POW emblem applied. Such was the significance towards *Hanoi Taxi* that the Air Force chose to allocate this historic aircraft to the National Museum of the US Air Force at Wright-Patterson. During February 2001, the aircraft was repainted in a similar white scheme from the historic mission's era and operated in this unique fashion until becoming the final Starlifter in service. A special ceremony at Wright-Patterson on May 6, 2006, officially retired the type from service, and transferred ownership to the museum.

The 375th Aeromedical Airlift Wing at Scott AFB, Illinois, also supported Operation *Homecoming*. At least one Douglas C-9A Nightingale sortie was flown into Hanoi. Furthermore, C-9As flew from four hubs to deliver some 591 returnees to air bases across the mainland US. One mission, which was part of the operation but not related to Vietnam, involved a crew from 18th MAS, 438th MAW at McGuire AFB. On March 13, 1973, the People's Republic of China released a POW from the Korean War period, following the direct intervention of President Nixon. John T Downey, who, despite being a CIA employee, was merely a passenger on a flight during the Korean War, when the aircraft was

Left: 63rd MAW C-141A 67-0007 flew twice from Hanoi to Clark, and four times from the Philippines to the US with repatriated ex-POWs. (PMC)

Below: During first the sortie to return the POWs from Hanoi in 1973, the repatriated personnel signed the large panel above the engineer's station on 66-0177. In addition to their names, some personnel included their period in captivity, and the aircraft type they were flying when captured. (USAF)

437th MAW C-141A 64-0618 landing at Aviano AB, Italy, in August 1980. Seven years earlier, the aircraft was the only 21st Air Force Starlifter to be involved in Operation *Homecoming*, transporting one POW urgently from Clark AB to the US on March 13, 1973. The C-141 was the only *Homecoming* aircraft not to be marked with the red cross on the tail. (Sergio Gava)

shot down by the North. After 20 years in a Chinese prison, and with his mother seriously ill, Nixon managed to obtain his release. Downey was taken to the border with Hong Kong, where a British representative took him to the international airport. A C-9A flew him to Clark AB, where 437th MAW C-141A 64-0618 flew him the 10.6hrs to Elmendorf AFB. A second crew then continued the journey to Connecticut and home.

This single sortie was ironic, as the 22nd Air Force was adamant that their units would fly all of the Operation *Homecoming* missions, to the detriment of their East Coast-based 21st Air Force counterpart. However, a 438th MAW crew was in the right place at the right time, and as such was included in the historic mission. Furthermore, the aircraft that they flew was a 437th MAW jet from Charleston AFB, meaning that two East Coast units were involved.

Follow-On Testing

Following the completion of the initial test and evaluation program at Edwards AFB, Starlifters 61-2775, -2776, -2777 and -2779 were retained by AFSC. They relocated to ASD between 1967 and mid-1971. Gradually, these aircraft were redesignated as NC-141As, beginning in late 1970. This reflected their role as permanently assigned to test and development work. The fuselage capacity was ideal for the installation and carriage of test equipment, sensors, and operators within large cargo hold. These programs were numerous, with many involving apparatuses being fitted, and key technicians carried during missions. Other, larger programs resulted in the fuselage being modified with external sensors and fairings.

Right: Suitably inscribed "First of the Fleet December 17th, 1963" to mark when NC-141A 61-2775 performed its maiden flight. (Don Crook)

Below: NC-141A 61-2775 of the Aeronautical Systems Division (ASD) at Wright-Patterson AFB in August 1970 in the all-silver scheme adopted by AFSC for a limited period. Note the extended nose probe. (Jack Morris)

61-2775, named the *First of the Fleet*, was redesignated as a JC-141A on March 31, 1964. It reverted to a C-141A on May 31, 1967, before becoming an NC-141A on December 25, 1969. It transferred to ASD on December 12, 1969. The majority of test functions were internal, with no additional exterior features. However, during 1997 and 1998, the aircraft was modified with a 1,000ft tow rope anchored firmly to the rear of the cargo floor. The other end of the tow line was attached to the nose of QF-106A 59-0130 for Project Eclipse. The project was sponsored by NASA's Dryden Flight Research Center. The first successful tow flight took place on December 20, 1997. The F-106 was simulating a future orbiter, which would be towed to a high altitude and released to fire its own engines and carry a payload into space. Six sorties were planned, before the program was terminated on February 6, 1998. This was the last project for 61-2775, as the aircraft was withdrawn 18 days later, and displayed at the Air Mobility Command Museum at Dover AFB.

61-2776 was named *Desert Rat* after having participated in the First Gulf War, and spending much time deployed at desert locations. It was another testbed, which performed much of its development work with equipment fitted internally. It evaluated fly-by-wire flight control systems, including a 1,000-hour demonstration program to obtain reliability data on the new all-electric system. Sorties included overseas destinations to assess the technology within a variety of meteorological environs. It was known by personnel at Edwards AFB as the Electric Starlifter. The aircraft visited Mildenhall during August 1997 and remained there for three weeks, before returning to the US. This was a rare European visit, and it was also in the UK during June 1997, visiting Brize Norton and Lakenheath.

61-2777 was named *The Gambler*. It was used in an early program to evaluate the ability to land on unpaved dirt runways, as well as steel matting laid on top of soil. In 1985, 61-2777 was extensively modified to flight test the Tail Warning Capability for the Rockwell B-1B and later the Northrop B-2. This program required the addition of a large fairing mounted at the rear fuselage to house the AN/ALQ-161 defensive avionics system. Another program involved the installation of a large sideways looking airborne radar mounted on the port side, just aft of the crew access door.

In keeping with the trend, 61-2779 was named *Against the Wind* by crew chief Paul Laemers, an avid Bob Seger fan. The most prominent feature was the extended pointed nose, for the Electronic Counter-Countermeasures Advanced Radar Test Bed program. Installed within the nose cones were advanced radar systems for the B-1B, F-15 Eagle, and GD F-16 Fighting Falcon.

Desert Rat, NC-141A 61-2776, making at rare visit to Mildenhall in August 1997. (Bob Archer)

Above: Seen in 1981, NC-141A 61-2777, with the ASD at Wright-Patterson AFB, is fitted with the sideways-looking radar on the forward fuselage and the giant tail extension. (Ben Knowles)

Right: NC-141A 61-2777 was cut into sections during February 2004, ready for road transportation to the HVF West scrap yard. (Bob Shane)

Above left: NC-141A 61-2779 in store for the AFFTC museum at Edwards AFB. Note the name, *Against the Wind*. (PMC)

Above right: C-141A 61-2779 is at Edwards AFB in June 1965 with a small parachutist on the nose. The aircraft had spent a period of time being evaluated with the 6511th Test Group (Parachute) at Naval Air Station (NAS) El Centro, California. (AFFTC)

Above left: Nose inscriptions and markings on NC-141A 61-2777 *The Gambler*. The crew have embellished the retirement date of "27 Sept 1994", with the significantly small flight hours total of "5254.3," the lowest in the fleet. (Doug Slowiak)

Above right: Weathered after a long period stored at Edwards AFB, NC-141A 61-2779 named *Against the Wind*, now displayed at the base museum. (via Paul Bennett)

An earlier test involved the installation of a Laser Infrared Countermeasures Demonstration System, to counter infrared guided missile threats. A low power chemical laser was mounted in the aft fuselage and fired through an aft port. Despite successful tests, the system was abandoned when funding was terminated.

The first three aircraft were pre-production examples, with subtle differences from the remainder. It is for this reason that 61-2779 remained designated as a C-141A until early in 1988, when the aircraft finally added to N prefix – this contradicts most other references.

Operational C-141s flew between 35,000 and 45,000 hours each, with C-141B 65-0251 being the fleet high flyer, accumulating 46,732 hours during 35 years of service. In contrast, the NC-141As flew between 5,254 and 9,607 hours.

DC-141A Proposal

On April 3, 1965, a memorandum was sent from James A Cunningham, Acting Assistant Director, Special Activities to the Deputy Director for Science and Technology concerning the USAF follow-on drone program. A proposal was being sought for the purchase of 50 reconnaissance drones, to be operated by five Air Force squadrons. The plan was for each squadron to be assigned two C-141As

Not all Starlifters survived into old age. 438th MAW C-141B 67-0017 had barely completed conversion when it burned out on the ground at McEntire ANGB, South Carolina, on March 7, 1982. (USAF)

modified for drone launch. If implemented, the program was to be operational as early as 1967. Understandably, the expensive program would be in direct competition with the Central Intelligence Agency TAGBOARD D-21. Seemingly, the proposal did not proceed beyond the memorandum, and therefore, the drone launch DC-141 mothership remained just a fascinating idea!

Other equally ambitious programs were considered for the Starlifter, including an airborne command post, aerial tanker, communications platform, an airborne spacecraft tracker and relay station, and even an airborne warning and control in place of the Boeing E-3 Sentry. Unfortunately, none of these proceeded past being an idea in a company brochure.

C-141B

Lockheed had originally proposed that the C-141 could be air refueled, although, at the time, the USAF did not consider this to be important. However, when fully loaded, the Starlifter was often required to land and refuel on lengthy trips, which was time consuming and inconvenient. Therefore, when the Lockheed proposal added this feature above the forward fuselage, along with the fuselage extension, it really was too good an offer to refuse.

The primary reason for this additional feature was Operation *Nickel Grass* during the fall of 1973, which was the response to the Arab invasion of Israel. The US operation to bolster Israel with replacement and additional weapons involved a reported 567 sorties by Lockheed C-5 Galaxies and C-141s. Not only was landing into a war zone difficult enough, but the refusal by both France and West Germany to allow MAC airlifters destined for Israel to refuel in their countries only compounded the issue. To resolve the refueling matter, airlifters utilized Lajes Field, Azores. MAC planners soon began to look to the future, and the lack of aerial refueling capability. Therefore, the proposal was included in the conversion proposal of the C-141A to B standard.

August 28, 1976 was a tragic day for the 438th MAW, when two of their C-141As were lost in separate accidents, both flying to European destination. 67-0008 crashed during landing at Sondrestrom AB, Greenland, while sister aircraft, 67-0006, was struck by lightning at Thorney, Cambridgeshire, England. 67-0008 is seen at Mildenhall in August 1974. (Bob Archer)

The company received a contract in May 1975 to modify all surviving MAC C-141As. At the time, this numbered 274 airframes, although two were subsequently lost, resulting in the total being reduced to 272. Those that were not modified were the four NC-141As, and 63-8077, 64-0641, 65-0274, 65-0281, 65-9407, 66-0127, 67-0006 and 67-0008, which were all lost in accidents before they could be converted.

The project was given the program name Pacer Plug, with a 13ft 4in (4.1m) extension being added in front of the wing and 10ft (3m) aft. This enabled a further three pallets to be carried and gave the USAF the equivalent of an additional 90 C-141As. The prototype YC-141B 66-0186 completed its first flight on March 25, 1977, before carrying out company trials. The aircraft was reassigned to the AFFTC for evaluation late in 1979. For the purposes of that assignment, the MAC tail band was changed to the Center's solid blue stripe containing a dozen white Xs.

Left: Having gained an aerial refueling receiver, the task of evaluating the new capability was carried out by the AFFTC at Edwards AFB. Here, YC-141B 66-0186 is about to connect with the flying boom of NKC-135A 55-3135. (AFFTC)

Below: 443rd MAW C-141B 64-0623 takes off at Dobbins AFB in June 1980 after completing conversion from C-141A standard. The two extension plugs are clearly visible in primer before its repainting. (R E Kling)

The initial operational example was 66-0176, which first flew on February 27, 1979, and was returned to Charleston AFB on December 4, 1979. The 100th C-141B conversion was 438th MAW 66-0126, which arrived at Marietta in December 1980 to begin the process. The 200th was 64-0639, which was awaiting return to service in early November 1981. The final aircraft was 63-8076, which was completed on June 29, 1982.

Above: **YC-141B 66-0186 briefly wore the AFFTC tail stripe of a blue band containing a dozen white Xs. The AFSC emblem is on the forward fuselage. Seen here at Edwards AFB in October 1979. (Mike Grove)**

Right: **The AFFTC tail band on YC-141B 66-0186 in September 1979 (Mike Grove)**

Chapter 3

Antarctica

The USAF had conducted resupply operations to the Antarctic continent since October 1956 under Operation *Deep Freeze*. From that period, the C-124 was the primary airlifter to land on the ice compacted runway at McMurdo Sound. The C-141A began to fly there from November 14, 1966, when 60th MAW 65-0229 successfully landed, proving Starlifter resupplies to the Antarctic were feasible. Some missions involved a landing, while others were simply air dropping supplies from low level to the more remote locations.

The small window of improved weather conditions, known as the austral summer, was from the period from November onwards. In readiness for flights to begin at that time, supplies were prepared

Above: **62nd MAW C-141A 65-0229 overflying near Mount McKinley in Washington State. This aircraft pioneered Antarctic operations, becoming the first Starlifter to land at McMudro Sound on November 14, 1966. (USAF)**

Left: **Shortly before engine start at McMurdo Sound, 452nd AW C-141C 65-0248 is preparing to return to Christchurch, New Zealand. (USAF)**

on pallets at Christchurch, New Zealand, to be unloaded at McMurdo Sound. Other cargoes were fitted with parachutes, for low level delivery to sites where landing was not possible. For these sorties, the aircrew would make contact with personnel at the site, where a flare would be ignited to enable the wind direction to be determined. The pilot would make a low fly-past of the area before the final run. With the rear petal doors open, the loadmaster and other crew members would push the load out into the slipstream, where the parachutes quickly opened, enabling the supplies to safely land near to the site buildings.

The initial Starlifter sortie encountered no problems, with the aircrew reporting that the departure was achieved in less than half of the runway length at McMurdo Sound. *Deep Freeze 68* was the last to involve MAC C-124s and C-130Es, as the following year was the first occasion when the C-141 performed all sorties. MAC's 21st Air Force selected the 438th MAW at McGuire AFB as much of the cargo to be ferried to Christchurch originated at NAS Quonset Point, Rhode Island. This included spare parts and other supplies for the Navy's Antarctic Development Squadron Six (VXE-6) whose LC-130 Hercules flew throughout the austral summer.

Two 438th MAW aircraft supported *Deep Freeze 69*, beginning on October 29, 1968. Subsequently, the Wing was the primary unit through to *Deep Freeze 74*. By this time, VXE-6 had relocated to NAS Point Mugu, California. The move also prompted MAC to reassign the mission to the 22nd Air Force. *Deep Freeze 75* was supported by two C-141As of the 60th MAW from Travis AFB. The 60th continued the role with the C-141A until *Deep Freeze 81*, when the B model was introduced. In the meantime, the sophistication of the C-141 enabled additional resupply deliveries to be planned. Known as *Ice Drop*, the first took place during July 1979, when a 63rd MAW C-141A made five passes over McMurdo Sound to extract 24 containers, which were all successfully recovered. The mission set the stage for further *Ice Drops* to be made each year.

The 619th Military Airlift Support Squadron at Hickam AFB organized Operating Location – Delta to coordinate activities at Christchurch. The 60th AMW flew the first of a new mission termed *Winter Fly-In*, abbreviated to *WINFLY*. Staged during August and September each year, *WINFLY* preceded the main season deliveries, with personnel and equipment to organize the sea ice runway, as well as any urgent requirements. These began in August 1996. The 60th relinquished the C-141 soon afterwards, with the 62nd AW beginning the mission the following year. During *Deep Freeze 90*, the 60th had trialed using the C-5A, which also proved successful. The C-17A was added for *Deep Freeze 1999–00* with a single 62nd AW aircraft beginning operations on October 15, 1999.

452nd AMW C-141C 67-0015 unloads cargo at McMurdo Sound during an Operation *Deep Freeze* mission. (USAF)

 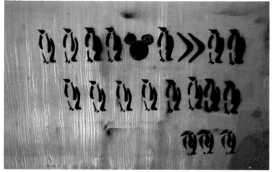

Above left: Nose markings of 452nd AMW C-141C 66-0151, with 18 penguin symbols, two boomerangs, and a Mickey Mouse applied during missions to Antarctica for Operation *Deep Freeze* in 2004. This was the last southern hemisphere season for the aircraft, as it was retired on July 19, 2004. (Woodie Hall)

Above right: Close-up of the Antarctica mission marks on C-141C 66-0151. (Woodie Hall)

Air Force Reserve Command had supported *Deep Freeze* for many years, augmenting active-duty crews. Beginning with *WINFLY 2001*, the Command began using their own aircraft on Antarctic missions. The 452nd AMW, flying the C-141C, initiated AFRC operations and was joined by the 445th AW from *Deep Freeze 2003–04*. However, Starlifter missions ceased on February 4, 2005, when the season finished and the aircraft returned home. The final sortie was performed by 452nd AMW C-141C 66-0152. Subsequent missions were exclusive to the C-17A. For almost the entire career of the Starlifter, the type supported the operation to this most hazardous of regions. It did so with no major mishaps, which is a testament to the crews, as well as the aircraft itself.

452nd AW C-141C 66-0152 is unloading at McMurdo Sound during a *Deep Freeze* mission. To ensure the aircraft do not suffer any systems icing up during the brief unloading period, heaters were used to blow hot air on certain areas, including the undercarriage. (USAF)

Supersonic Starlifter?

A story has been circulating within the Starlifter community that 63rd MAW C-141A 65-9402 may well have exceeded the sound barrier during 1976. While cruising at 39,000ft (11,887m) and without warning, the aircraft swung sharply to the right. The pilot disconnected the autopilot and yaw damper. The Dutch Roll became worse, and the pilot started a descent and regained control at 31,000ft (9,449m). After the aircraft landed, the number 2 and 3 yaw damper rate gyros were replaced, and the write-up signed off.

The next day, while returning to home base, cruising at 41,000ft (12,497m), the crew felt a couple of small jolts. They disconnected the autopilot and waited. After a few moments, when nothing more was felt, they reconnected it. Moments later, the nose slammed violently to the right. The pilot again disconnected the autopilot and yaw damper. He attempted to control the Dutch Roll with aileron. Within seconds, the aircraft was partially inverted. The rolling and yawing continued as pitch reached 90° nose down. Loose objects flew around the cockpit, with the crew bunk mattresses and the navigator lying across the instrument panel, hindering vision and control movements.

The pilot regained control and recovered from the high-speed dive at 17,000ft (5,182m). The crew performed a controllability check and recovered the aircraft to the nearest military base, RCAFB Comox in Canada. Large pieces of the upper wing skin and parts of both petal doors were missing. Flight recorder data indicated 'g' loadings of +3.18 to -3.52 and a maximum of 450kts indicated airspeed. Investigators were unable to confirm the maximum Mach but suspect it had exceeded Mach 1.0. They found that the aircraft had experienced seven yaw related flight control malfunctions. The dual malfunction of the autopilot junction box and the yaw damper control panel caused intermittent spurious signals to the yaw damper, yet gave a satisfactory test indication after the first incident. Following repairs, the aircraft resumed routine duties.

The supersonic Starlifter 65-9402, seen taxiing here at Rhein Main, West Germany, with the 438th MAW in 1970. It transferred to the 63rd MAW by 1976, when the aircraft is believed to have achieved this significant milestone unintentionally. (Peter Zastrow)

Operations *Desert Shield* and *Desert Storm*

The second largest commitment for the Starlifter and its crews – the biggest being the Vietnam War – was Operation *Desert Shield* during the second half of 1990. Organized in seemingly record time, the priority airlift by hundreds of aircraft to the Middle East can best be described at frenetic. Throughout the first few weeks of the campaign, C-141s flew daily from a host of locations across the United States to the Middle East, known as the Area of Responsibility. A MAC press release gave an insight into the buildup of US forces, from a handful of advisers in the region in early August, to a personnel level numbering 525,000 by the time the ground war started in February 1991.

Not only was it necessary to ferry the majority of these personnel by air halfway around the world, but having completed their journey, they had to be housed, fed and resupplied. Urgently needed tanks and armor, together with the munitions to be used, were also delivered quickly. Furthermore, the squadrons of tactical aircraft being rapidly deployed from their home stations also needed their ground support and weaponry to be in place upon arrival. While a considerable volume of follow-on equipment could be delivered by sea, the initial requirements could not take the slow route. Eventually, US personnel were located at dozens of sites across the region, ranging from huge air bases to small concentrations.

MAC claimed the air and sealift to be the one of biggest in history. While significantly smaller than the Berlin Airlift in the number of aircraft flown, the *Desert Shield* build up was much larger in the tonnage of cargo carried. MAC stated that the same total volume transported during the entire Berlin Airlift was moved in the equivalent of just the first 22 days of *Desert Shield*.

The first MAC C-141 mission to the Middle East was 67-0016 of 437th MAW on August 7, from Charleston AFB to Dhahran AB with Airlift Control Elements (ACE) teams. ACE personnel were established at facilities across the US as well as at Middle Eastern destination bases. The teams brought expertise in loading techniques, departure preparations, and unloading procedures for arrivals. Teams were composed of logistics specialists who had the knowledge and proficiency to accomplish mass movements of personnel and equipment.

US Air Force tactical units, such as the 1st TFW McDonnell F-15 Eagles, were flown nonstop from Langley AFB, Virginia, to Saudi Arabia. While KC-135s performed a tanker air bridge for the Eagles, MAC airlifters ferried technicians and other support personnel, plus everything necessary for the unit to turn the jets around soon after arrival and begin patrols. The US Army also dispatched a sizeable portion both the 82nd and 101st Airborne Divisions from Fort Bragg, North Carolina, and Fort Campbell, Kentucky, respectively, beginning in the first half of August 1990 – utilizing

Two crew members shade under 438th MAW C-141B 67-0007 at Dhahran AB during *Desert Shield*. (USAF)

306 C-141 and 155 C-5 sorties, plus commercial airliners. A similar situation occurred with many other Army, Air Force, Navy and Marine Corps elements, hurriedly readied at their home stations for a potentially open-ended commitment in the Middle East. The Starlifter was at the forefront of moving all these forces.

At any given time, a small percentage of the C-141 fleet was undertaking major overhaul at the Warner Robins Air Logistics Center (ALC) at Robins AFB. Each complete overhaul required the removal of all external paint, to inspect the bare metal surface for corrosion. Known as Inspect and Repair as Necessary (IRAN), and later Planned Depot Maintenance (PDM), the refurbishment, including a complete repaint, could take many days to complete. However, such was the need for every available asset, that a small number of C-141Bs were returned to service in natural metal finish. These Starlifters resumed tasking without the niceties of being painted – that could wait until things quieted down.

According to crew chief Robert Stemple, 4950th Test Wing NC-141As 61-2775 and 61-2776 were involved in the resupply effort during the Gulf campaign. Such was the need for airlifter capability, that two largely unmodified pre-production Starlifters were available for a short period to carry much needed cargo from the US for the Middle East. Stemple also stated that both aircraft achieved a very credible 97 percent reliability rate. Being preproduction A models, the seconded active-duty aircrews found the NC-141s somewhat antiquated.

The military established a system nicknamed the "aluminum bridge," for the C-5, C-41, as well as the McDonnell Douglas KC-10A and Boeing KC-135. Crews were positioned at major en-route airlift hubs, such as Torrejón and Zaragoza, Spain, Ramstein and Rhein Main, Germany, and to a lesser degree, Mildenhall and Upper Heyford, UK. An aircraft on a flight from the US to the Middle East would land at one of these en route bases, where a fresh crew would continue with the second leg of the journey following refueling. This was the same stage system that was so successful during the Vietnam War. However, the flying time from Charleston AFB to Dhahran AB, for example, was approximately 17hrs – this being half the time from Travis AFB to Saigon during the Vietnam War. Destination air bases in Bahrain, Oman, Saudi Arabia, and the UAE had no parking spaces available for crew rest. Therefore, it became necessary for crews to depart as soon as the cargo and passengers had deplaned and fly largely empty to one of the European airlift hubs. Workdays were routinely extended well above the peacetime norm.

438th MAW C-141B 64-0627, landing at Mildenhall in April 1991, was one of approximately half a dozen aircraft that hurriedly completed Planned Depot Maintenance (PDM) and returned to service before repainting. Such was the massive requirement for airlift during *Desert Shield* and *Desert Storm*. (Bob Archer)

An unknown 62nd MAW pilot proudly standing adjacent to artwork of Mickey Mouse riding a camel, and the inscription "Mickey's Desert Express" on C-141B 65-0263. (62nd MAW)

By October 1990, a serious backlog of urgently needed spare parts began to emerge. To rectify the situation, MAC instigated the Desert Express (DE) on October 30, designed to ensure next day delivery of any cargoes highlighted as critical to the potential war effort. A further two daily flights, known as European Desert Express (EE), were added on December 8, as the buildup continued. All Defense Department services utilized these flights, which were successful, as they were given a high priority.

445th AW 64-0637 was one of 40-plus AFRC Starlifters that were in temporary residence at Mildenhall during the opening stages of Second Gulf War. After an all too short period, the operation was relocated to Ramstein. (Bob Archer)

The C-141 exclusively flew 135 DE missions until May 20, 1991, and 92 EE sorties until March 14, 1991, when these were discontinued. DE sorties originated at Charleston AFB, with a guarantee that cargo or passengers would be in Saudi Arabia within 24 hours. Turn-around at either Torrejón or Zaragoza, for example, would often be within one hour, with a fresh crew departing for their final destination. EE started at Rhein Main each day.

Understandably, the C-141 was most numerous of the dedicated strategic airlift fleet, and quickly became known as the workhorse of *Desert Shield* and *Desert Storm*. Starlifters flew 8,536 strategic airlift missions, followed by the C-5 with 3,770, the KC-10A with 379 and the C-9 with 209. The C-141 and C-5 accounted for 361,147 tons, or 66 percent of the cargo airlifted in support of the Gulf War.

The frantic pace of Starlifter operations can best be summed up by more official figures. In mid-August 1990, MAC had 195 of their 266 Starlifters committed to *Desert Shield* – 23 others were dedicated to additional priority missions, while 48 more were in various maintenance groups. Normal C-141 peacetime mission rate was 500 per month, but, by December 1990, this had soared to 1,400! Despite the end of hostilities, following the liberation of Kuwait, the continued presence of Saddam Hussein in a smaller area of Iraq required a sizeable coalition presence in the region. Therefore, the C-141 was involved in the resupply of forces in the Gulf region and Turkey.

Operations - Gulf War II

The Second Gulf War, which commenced in March 2003, was the final fully fledged combat operation involving the C-141. Whereas the majority of Starlifter resupply operations in *Desert Shield* and *Desert Storm* were between the US and the Middle East, this was changed for the second campaign. AFRC C-141C squadrons were forward deployed to Europe with operations centralized at RAF Mildenhall initially, but later relocated to Ramstein AB. Almost every one of the 45 or so AFRC Starlifters was involved, ferrying supplies between European hubs and various Middle Eastern bases. For many of the aircraft, this was their swansong, as they were retired for storage a short time after being released from the campaign.

C-141C 66-0177 of the 445th AW during a sortie to Mildenhall in February 2003, while supporting Gulf War Two. (Bob Archer)

Chapter 4

Reserves

A ir Force Reserve (AFRes) squadrons had traditionally operated their own aircraft until the arrival of the C-141A with active duty. With the desire to man the new Starlifter with AFRes aircrews and maintenance personnel, but with insufficient aircraft for direct assignment, an innovative plan was established. Under the pioneering Associate program, reservists crewed and maintained aircraft assigned to active-duty units. The initiative enabled squadrons to reduce full-time personnel while still fulfilling their assigned flying program. The first reserve unit to fly the Starlifter was the 326th MAS (Associate) at Dover AFB beginning on September 25, 1968.

The Associate program was extended to six numbered Military Airlift Groups, which were replaced by five numbered Wings in July 1973. The success of the Starlifter flown and maintained by reservists lead to aircraft being directly assigned when sufficient numbers of C-17s had been delivered to active duty. These commenced assignment in July 1986 when the 756th MAS at Andrews AFB, Maryland, and the 183rd MAS, Mississippi ANG at Jackson Airport both began the transition. The two squadrons received a complement of eight (later nine) Starlifters and were the only such reservist units until April 1992 when the 155th AS/Tennessee ANG switched from the C-130 Hercules. Two more AFRes units transitioned to the C-141 – 445th Airlift Wing (AW) at Wright-Patterson AFB in March 1993 and the 452nd AMW at March AFB one month later. On February 17, 1997, AFRes was renamed Air Force Reserve Command (AFRC). All reservist C-141Bs were upgraded to C-141C standard beginning in October 1997.

Having just completed conversion to C-141C standard, Mississippi ANG Starlifter 64-0614 awaits delivery at Waco's Tsti Airport back to Jackson International Airport (IAP). (Keith Snyder)

C-141C

Emerging technology did not have a significant impact upon the Starlifter until the latter part of the aircraft's career. The introduction of digital cockpit modernization persuaded the Air Force to fund a limited program to improve 63 C-141Bs exclusively for the reserves. The seven reserve squadrons each had nine aircraft, hence 63 modifications. Raytheon E-Systems was contracted to upgrade the aircraft to C-141C standard with a new flight control system, traffic control avoidance system (TCAS) linked to a GPS Enhanced navigation system, and an updated aircraft self-protection system. The first modified aircraft was 65-9414 from the 452nd AMW at March ARB, which was converted by the Warner Robins ALC, and was returned to service on October 31, 1997. (Note – March was an Air Force Base until April 1, 1996, when changed to an Air Reserve Base.) The remainder were modified by Raytheon E-Systems at their facility at Tsti Airport in Waco, Texas. Aircraft for the reserves were selected as these were expected to be in service longer than those of the active duty. Despite the investment, Mississippi ANG C-141C 64-0632 was retired to AMARC (Aircraft Maintenance and Regeneration Center) on

Right: Proudly displaying the emblem of the 4th Allied POW Wing, C-141C 66-0177 commemorates what was possibly the most significant mission in Military Aircraft Command (MAC) history. (PMC)

Below: Nine months after completing conversion to become the first C-141C, 65-9414 of the 452nd AMW is at Fairford in July 1998. The aircraft was the only one completed at Warner Robins Air Logistics Complex (ALC), as the remainder were modified at Waco's Tsti Airport. (Bob Archer)

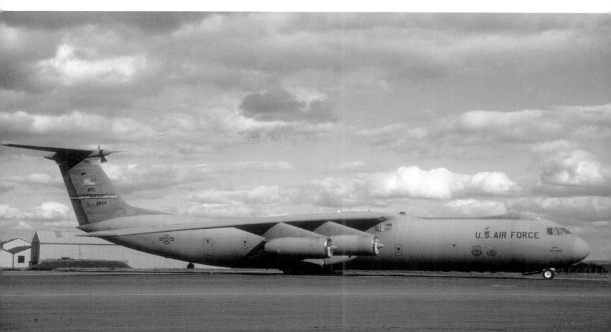

The result of an unfortunate accident in which C-141C 61-2778 suffered the port wing collapsing when over pressurized during refueling. The accident on December 21, 2001 at Memphis IAP, caused the aircraft to fall to starboard, damaging that wing also. Due to imminent retirement, the aircraft was not repaired. (Mark Baker)

December 3, 2002, after only four years' service. The remainder followed, apart from 61-2778, which was the only C model to be destroyed when a fuel tank was over pressurized, resulting in the port wing collapsing. Additionally, 66-0177 was retired to the National Museum of the US Air Force.

Specialist Assignment 1 – SOLL II

The Special Operations Low Level (SOLL) mission was originally developed following the ill-fated attempt to rescue American citizens from Tehran, Iran, in April 1980. Operation *Eagle Claw* was a failure, and lead to a review of special operations, particularly those likely to take place in nations hostile towards the US. The C-130 Hercules and Starlifter were amongst the fixed-wing types highlighted for a demanding role assisting Special Forces. The SOLL I was flown by C-130s expressly for daylight low-level operations, while SOLL II was epitomized for flying at night. SOLL I evolved into the various MC-130 programs operated by AF Special Operations Command. The C-141B assumed the SOLL II mission in 1983, assigned to the 76th MAS at Charleston AFB. The 16th MAS replaced the 76th in October 1993. With the impending retirement of the C-141 at Charleston, the aircraft were transferred to the 6th AS at McGuire AFB in April 1999. The transfer ended their SOLL II mission on April 9, 1999, with the task being transferred to the C-17. However, the Starlifters retained the exterior sensors fit, probably in a backup capacity. SOLL II was also performed by the Lockheed C-5 Galaxy with the 436th MAW/AW. Gradually, the mission was taken over by the McDonnell C-17, with some 50 aircraft currently fitted with the required capability. Whereas the C-141s were distinguishable by their additional external sensors, the C-17s had these features as a standard fitting internally.

SOLL II was performed by 13 C-141Bs, serials 64-0630, 65-0224, 65-9401, 66-0131, 66-0155, 66-0192, 66-7947, 67-0003, 67-0004, 67-0010, 67-0013, 67-0014, and 67-0165. An elite cadre of aircrews were qualified for night vision low-level flying and fast cargo offload. The primary function was to rapidly deploy and insert special operations ground forces into blacked-out, austere airfields or drop zones, and to extract those forces when necessary. Additionally, air drops of Special Forces boats and personnel onto water were tasked, along with high and low altitude parachute insertion. These missions were similar to those performed by the MC-130s, but the specialized C-141s were able to carry more troops or cargo over greater distances. Activities were coordinated through the Special Operations Division of the parent Wing.

437th AW C-141B 66-0131, with additional nose antennae for the SOLL II mission, outside the Warner Robins ALC at Robins AFB in July 1992. It was repainted soon afterwards in the AMC Proud Gray scheme. (L.B.Sides)

By April 1999, C-141B 66-0131 had received a slightly more attractive external finish, and a colorful tail stripe. Seen here landing at Mildenhall. (Andy Thomson)

Arguably the ugliest color scheme applied to the Starlifter. C-141B 67-0020 was one of the four Joint Airborne Communications Center/Command Posts (JACC/CP) adapted to enable troop commanders being flown to a specific destination to be updated with the latest combat information. The upper fuselage has additional satellite communications antennae, which use different frequencies to those of the flight crew. Barely visible is the rear facing high frequency (HF) aerial positioned midway along the wing. (Doug Slowiak)

Various communications antennae are visible above and below the fuselage of 305th AMW SOLL II 67-0020 during October 1998. (PMC)

Each aircraft was especially outfitted with an enhanced suite of communications equipment, as well as a global positioning system. The cockpit lightning was compatible with the crew using night vision goggles. Initially, there were no external features, but 66-0131 is believed to have been modified and evaluated by Warner Robins ALC with a terrain following capability, as well as effective missile warning systems. The modification was first noted in July 1992. Following evaluation operationally, the Air Force funded a US$41m program to equip all 13 with these features. Directly beneath the nose was a turret for the Texas Instruments AN/AAQ-17 forward looking infrared (FLIR) imager which gave the aircraft the ability to "see in the dark." Imagery was displayed primarily on a console mounted on the navigator's station, as well as an auxiliary screen for the pilot. The navigator was responsible for guiding the FLIR system by means of a joystick. Other items included the AN/AAR-44 infrared missile-warning sensor fitted under the fuselage and an AN/ALR-69 radar-warning receiver with antennae on the nose and tail. Mounted each side of the nose were AN/ALE-40 chaff and flare dispensers, while similar systems were located on the main undercarriage wheel well covers, and the wing tips. The defensive countermeasures system could be set to automatic mode to dispense chaff and flares without crew activation, with the quantity of each preprogramed. The loadmaster could also activate dispensers while monitoring surface-to-air missile activity from the rear ramp. The latter additions were referred to as Special Operations Forces Improvement Modification (SOFI-Mod). The C-141 SOLL II aircraft were retired between July 10, 2000, and October 18, 2002.

Specialist Assignment 2 – Joint Airborne Communications Center/ Command Post

Four C-141Bs were modified with enhanced communications for a mission associated with the rapid deployment of forces. The Joint Airborne Communications Center/Command Post (JACC/CP) aircraft were assigned to the 438th MAW (305th AMW from October 1, 1994) at McGuire AFB. Three, and almost certainly all four, were upgraded to this standard during the summer and fall of 1981, when they were converted to C-141B. The aircraft involved were 64-0623, 65-0221, 67-0019, and 67-0020.

JACC/CP aircraft had enhanced communications capabilities which included satellite communication (SATCOM), secure voice radios, and teletype to link a joint task force commander with higher headquarters and other ground centers, while airborne. The aircraft were distinguishable by UHF/FM and VHF blade aerials aft of the flight-refueling receptacle and a pair of T-shaped

Right: Extra antennae can be seen on 438th AW JACC/CP C-141B 64-0623 at Pope AFB in April 1992. (Bob Archer)

Below: 65-0221, wearing a stylized color scheme for the JACC/CP role with the 438th AW, landing at Mildenhall in March 1993. (Bob Archer)

SATCOM antennae above the wing root. Rear-facing HF probe antennae were also mounted on the center section of the wings. Other small aerials were positioned along the lower fuselage. A JACC/CP module could be rolled into the aircraft and off-loaded at the destination and used in a ground mode. JACC/CP could connect up to 16 users on two platforms, with classified and unclassified messages transmitted through commercial internet and secure telephone systems.

Some of these aircraft retained the attractive white and gray paint scheme long after most others had been camouflaged. Little information has been released about this role, but it is believed to have been implemented due to the shortage of satellite communications during periods of high demand.

The plethora of additional communications antennae, as well as the HF aerial facing backwards on the wing point, on 305th AMW C-141B 64-0623. One of just four JACC/CP aircraft, it is seen departing Mildenhall in May 1997. (Bob Archer)

Long after the C-141B fleet had been repainted European One, those performing the JACC/CP mission retained the white/gray scheme. 65-0221 is seen at Aviano AB in January 1991. (Sergio Gava)

Following the retirement of the modified Starlifters, JACC/CP is now a feature of the C-17A. Whereas the JACC/CP C-141 was distinguishable by additional antennae, the C-17 fleet has these already installed, enabling all aircraft to be mission capable. The 314th TAW at Little Rock AFB, Arkansas, had C-130Es compatible with the system, from at least 1983.

Seconds from Disaster – 64-0638 over N'Djamena

The C-141 flew daily embassy courier flights around the world, often landing at civilian airports close to the capital being supported by the US military. Diplomatic clearance was ordinarily arranged beforehand, with the aircrew briefed of arrangements in place to ensure the mission proceeded as

438th MAW C-141B 64-0638 at McGuire AFB in March 1985. Thirty months later, after the aircraft had been camouflaged, it was seconds from being shot down over Chad by French Mirage F.1C fighters. The French mistakenly identified the Starlifter as a Libyan Il-76. (Don Spering)

smoothly as possible. During September 1987, 438th MAW C-141B 64-0638 was scheduled to be flown by a crew (reported to be from 63rd MAW at Norton AFB) on a multi-stop embassy run across central Africa. The mission originated at Charleston AFB with a refueling stop in Bermuda, before crossing the Atlantic Ocean to land at Dakar. Next destinations were Roberts Field, Liberia; Kinshasa, Democratic Republic of Congo; Niamey, Niger; Kinshasa again, before returning to Bermuda, and Charleston.

Prior to departing Dakar, the crew attempted to confirm the diplomatic clearance for their next destinations but was only partially successful. They elected to continue as planned, and to complete the final arrangements for Niger via the MAC command and control system. Assuming everything

Devoid of military markings when supporting the Organizacion Meteorologica Mundial – Naciones Unidas (World Meteorological Organization – United Nations) at Acapulco Airport, Mexico, in July 1980. (Gary Baker collection)

was in order, the flight from Kinshasa to Niamey on September 10 proceeded, which involved skirting southwest Chad. Unbeknownst to the crew, France had intervened in the Chad–Libya war in 1987, with restricted air traffic over Chad. No aerial traffic was allowed in an area that extended from the 16th parallel to the outskirts of the capital N'Djamena.

During the summer of 1987, Libyan Tupolev Tu-22s, along with Ilushin Il-76 cargo aircraft loaded with pallets of bombs, had attacked towns near the 16th parallel in the area of Faya-Largeau. On September 7, a French Raytheon MIM-23B HAWK surface-to-air missile had shot down a Libyan Tu-22 over N'Djamena. Understandably, the French were very twitchy of any unidentified aircraft, and immediately went on alert when the C-141 appeared unannounced from the south. Unable to make radio contact, and assuming this was another Libyan IL-76 raid, two Mirage F.1Cs on patrol were vectored to intercept. Having established visual identification on the intruder, the Mirage lead pilot confirmed the aircraft to be an IL-76 and armed his missiles. The second fighter pilot doubted the visual identification, and flew closer, confirming that it was a camouflaged USAF C-141. He quickly advised his leader to counter the missile lock. The C-141 pilot was subsequently instructed to land at N'Djamena Airport. It transpired that the American crew had not read the airspace restriction notice.

The Mirage pilot advised the American crew that they had been just a few seconds from being on the receiving end of an air-to-air missile, which would have destroyed the Starlifter and crew. An investigation revealed that the diplomatic clearances provided to the C-141 crew were more than two years old! Successive instructions to aircrews flying embassy supply flights to this part of Africa were advised to remain well clear of the restricted zone.

United Nations Support

The Starlifter supported many government and scientific initiatives, including NASA and the National Oceanic and Atmospheric Administration (NOAA), as well as the United Nations for peacekeeping activities. Most of these support endeavors involved transporting personnel and equipment to sites around the world. For the majority of occasions, the aircraft retained their full military color scheme.

During July 1980, NASA's L-300 was to be deployed to Mexico for a joint UN, NASA and NOAA project. However, the Mexican government would not allow the support C-141s to carry military identity. Therefore, 60th MAW C-141As 63-8084 and 65-0252 had all traces of military ownership removed, with just the tail number remaining. The gray underside and white tail and upper surfaces were totally devoid of any insignia, apart from the United Nations emblem on the tail. Clearly the program was of sufficient importance to justify the cost and effort in completely de-militarizing the aircraft externally. One report suggests the joint NASA/NOAA project was organized by the Ames Laboratory and financially backed by the UN.

C-141A 65-0252 at Acapulco Airport in July 1980, while on loan to the United Nations. (Gary Baker collection)

Chapter 5

Starlifter Color Schemes

The C-141 fleet had four distinct color schemes throughout its 42 years of service. Details of the initial natural metal scheme were presented in chapter one. The regular long overwater sorties to Vietnam, combined with tropical weather conditions in SEA, reportedly caused corrosion along rivet lines. Whereas tactical aircraft were camouflaged, the C-141 was not considered to be within this category and, therefore, retained the natural metal finish throughout the majority of the campaign. To counter the corrosion issue, an attractive new airline style scheme was introduced in 1971. The upper surface and fin were painted gloss white, while the underside was a pale gray. All nationality, command, and unit details were applied in full color.

The Air Force has frequently adopted new patterns to adjust to emerging threats, with the Starlifter changing again to enable aircraft to merge into the European theater because of the perceived notion that a confrontation with the Soviet Union and the Warsaw Pact was a possibility. In 1979, 65-0270 was one of the first to be repainted in a two-tone dark green and slate gray camouflage. The majority of the fleet received this pattern, which was known as "European One." Lockheed Marietta was notified that all Starlifter conversions to B model would be repainted in the low visibility camouflage from December 22, 1980. Often referred to as the "lizard" scheme, all nationality markings and command insignia were applied in black outline form. Gradually, a little color began to appear, with specific Wing tail stripes becoming the norm.

437th MAW C-141A 65-0217 taking off in November 1978. Originally delivered to the 150st ATW before transferring to Charleston AFB for service with the 437th MAW. (PMC)

63rd MAW C-141A clearly shows the numerous circular metallic sections that were riveted together to form the aircraft. Frequent sorties across the Pacific Ocean reportedly caused corrosion along rivet lines, leading to the white upper/gray lower paint scheme. (PMC)

60th MAW C-141B 65-0234 during takeoff in April 1990, shortly before the aircraft was repainted in the European One camouflage. (PMC)

Completely anonymous-looking C-141A 65-0270 being crewed by 437th MAW personnel, at Rhein Main, date unknown. (Peter Zastrow)

However, the lizard pattern was not popular with aircrews as the dark colors retained heat, which was particularly uncomfortable when aircraft operated into hotter destinations. Furthermore, crew chiefs also did not favor the dark scheme, as there was a lack of individuality, with all aircraft looking the same. Aircraft were repainted in European One as they were cycled through planned depot maintenance at the Warner Robins ALC. Most were C-141Bs, although the camouflage was also applied to a small number of A models. However, a handful of specialist aircraft were spared the low visibility color. These included the four JACC/CP, and those which flew in the VIP role – all of which retained the white and gray scheme for many years.

Right: 67-0021 in June 1982 at McGuire with the blackjack playing cards on the nose. Note the 438th MAW has been covered by the 514th, although part of this has peeled off. The "#1 BPO" refers to the crew chief responsible for Basic Post-Flight Inspection of his particular aircraft. (via John Vadas)

Below: After a period of virtual anonymity, with black command and unit markings on the European One color scheme, units began to apply a colorful tail stripe. In the case of the 459th AW, this was a black and yellow check, containing the base name. 64-0620 is seen at Andrews AFB in October 1994. (Bruce Trombecky)

445th AW C-141C 66-7954 showing an area of the rear fuselage, which has either been washed or repainted. The Proud Gray scheme was difficult to keep clean. (Andy Thomson)

Clearly, the threat in Europe receded when the Cold War ended. By this time, low visibility dark colors were being replaced, with either a single or two-tone gray pattern being adopted. In the case of the Starlifter, the new scheme, known as Air Mobility Command Proud Gray, was evaluated during the summer of 1991. The new gray was soon adopted as aircraft emerged from major overhaul at the Warner Robins ALC.

The only two-tone gray C-141A 67-0021 overflying Nevada during evaluation of the scheme. Pattern was applied in 1977 and carried for three years. The USAF did not proceed with the idea, with the aircraft being repainted European One when modified to C-141B standard. (USAF)

MAC experimented with at least two different schemes, neither of which proceeded beyond the trials stage. One was a two-tone light gray pattern, which was applied to 438th MAW C-141A 67-0021 by October 1977. One source suggests the camouflage was known as Mask-10A, as it was based upon that applied to the Fairchild A-10A Thunderbolt II. An aircrew rumor suggested it may have been radar absorbent material, although this is unconfirmed. What is known is that the rough, almost sandpaper feel of the exterior surface, created more drag, increasing fuel consumption by approximately 15 percent. Furthermore, the paint scheme added considerable extra weight to the aircraft, which needed to be factored into statistics by aircrews. The aircraft flew with this camouflage until December 3, 1980, when conversion to the C-141B commenced and it was repainted in the European One scheme. A C-130E also flew in a similar pattern at the same time.

Right: **The unique two-tone gray C-141A 67-0021 lands at Mildenhall in October 1979. (Paul Bennett)**

Below: **C-141A 67-0021 receives some engine maintenance on the parking area adjacent to the main road running past RAF Mildenhall in April 1979. (Bob Archer)**

Forward fuselage and engine detail of C-141A 67-0021 at Mildenhall in April 1979. (Bob Archer)

The second camouflage pattern was applied to a pair of 63rd MAW C-141Bs, both of which had tan areas applied to their European One pattern. 65-9397 had small tan rectangles painted aft of the nose, along the fuselage, and across the leading edge of the wings. This additional color was seen in April 1983 but had gone by April 1984.

63rd MAW C-141B 65-9397 finished in European One, with small tan rectangles. Applied by April 1983, but removed the following year, the pattern was not adopted. (PMC)

Starboard side view of 63rd MAW 65-9397 with the additional tan rectangles on the fuselage and wings in April 1983. (PMC)

Sister C-141B 65-9404 was far more elaborately decorated. Applied over the lizard pattern were large areas of tan and pale gray. The finished result was extremely untidy and could not have been scruffier if the additional colors had been applied by a group of young children! Furthermore, the lighter colors naturally attracted dirt and grime that were left unwashed. The scheme was seen during the spring and summer of 1982 but had reverted to normal by October.

63rd MAW C-141B 65-9404 was repainted with a tan and gray pattern, although daubed would be a better description. The additional colors were added for tests in 1983. (John Gourley collection)

Determining the reason for the addition of the tan paint has not been easy, although a likely rationale would be that unease across the Middle East would have involved resupply by the United States to support their allies in the region. To enable airlifters to blend in with the desert surroundings during resupply sorties to allied nations such as Israel and others in the Persian Gulf, the USAF may have wished to apply a measure of desert paint to the otherwise dark aircraft pattern. A small number of C-130Es were also repainted in a full desert scheme. One source has suggested these C-141s were evaluated during exercises at Nellis AFB, Nevada, although their effectiveness would appear to have been minimal, as no further aircraft were repainted.

Bedecked with an extremely attractive VIP color scheme, C-141B 67-0166 is seen here during September 1993. The aircraft was retired to Scott AFB, with the intention of being exhibited at a proposed museum, but when this failed to materialize, the Starlifter was cut up for scrap early in 2020. (PMC)

Crew posing with VIP-configured C-141B 66-0199 while supporting one of Bob Hope's Middle East tours. Note the access steps to enable the entertainers to enter the jet, and the cartoon of Bob Hope on the fuselage. (Bob McDaniel)

Above left: C-141B 66-0199 was configured for distinguished visitors, including entertainer Bob Hope, whose caricature was applied to the forward fuselage especially for his European tour. (via Ben Knowles)

Above right: Entertainer Bob Hope emerging from a specially marked C-141B during one of his Christmas tours to the Middle East. (Kevin Roles)

As stated earlier, a small number of C-141Bs retained the white/gray scheme long after the fleet had received the European One pattern. These included the four JACC/CP aircraft, as well as 66-0186 and 67-0166, both of which served as the flagship for the four-star general commanding Military Airlift Command. Both had a removable VIP module installed to enable the "boss" to remain in communication even when on long distance flights. Another B model, serial 66-0199, retained the more attractive scheme, and was used for VIP support, including the annual Bob Hope tours to entertain the troops deployed overseas in combat theaters. 60th AW C-141B 65-0239 also retained the white pattern until late 1992, possibly also performing a VIP type role on behalf of the commander of the 22nd Air Force headquarters.

Proudly proclaiming "MAC One" on the VIP-configured steps, 66-0186 was one of two aircraft which were the primary form of transportation for the Commander-in-Chief of MAC for many years. It is here at Fairford in July 1985. (Bob Archer)

In the mid-1990s, 66-0186 was used by Lockheed to investigate the extent of fatigue cracking in the wings. Subsequently, it was parked in sections at Marietta for a number of years, to be an exhibit in a proposed museum. A dedicated team of former Starlifter technicians managed to source four engines from 67-0166 at Scott AFB, with a view to full restoration as the YC-141B. (via Milslides)

Another VIP C-141B, 438th AW 66-0199, lands at Mildenhall in March 1994. The VIP Starlifters retained the white color scheme long after others were either European One or AMC Proud Gray. This aircraft supported at least one Bob Hope tour of US forces deployed overseas in combat regions. (Bob Archer)

Above: 60th AW C-141B 65-0239, inscribed "The Forty Niners," lands at Yokota AB, Japan, in August 1992. No doubt, Travis personnel were supporters of the San Francisco team. (Masanori Ogawa)

Right: 60th AW C-141B 65-0239 named *The Forty Niners* during October 1992. The aircraft retained the white scheme long after the majority had been camouflaged, suggesting the VIP role. (Norman Graser)

Below: C-141B 66-0186 performing a VIP task to Andrews AFB during November 1990. (Charles B. Mayer)

Starlifter Additional Markings

Despite regulations laid down for color schemes, the ingenuity of personnel has seen individuality spring up on occasions. A small number of C-141s were given individual names, some of which were officially sanctioned, and were retained for long periods. Arguably, the best known was 63-8088, which was christened *The Golden Bear* ahead of becoming the first Starlifter to join an operational unit. The name was applied for the acceptance ceremony at Travis AFB, and, unusually, was painted on both sides of the nose. Furthermore, the name was retained for the entire operational period, and can still be seen as the aircraft is displayed at the base. Others had a much shorter lifespan. Some included elaborate and tasteful artwork, although most were simply a name applied in black.

More than 40 Starlifters were inscribed with names, including the following:

Named *Spirit of the Inland Empire*, 63rd MAW C-141B 63-8085 is seen here during October 1993. (PMC)

Forty-plus Starlifters were christened with inscriptions, including 60th MAW 65-0259 named *City of Fairfield*, a town adjacent to the air base. (Doug Slowiak)

Serial	Unit	Name
61-2775	AFFTC	*First of the Fleet*
61-2776	AFFTC	*Desert Rat*
61-2777	AFFTC	*The Gambler*
61-2778	TN ANG	*Father Time*
61-2779	AFFTC	*Against the Wind*
63-8075	AFFTC	*Petunia Pig*
63-8075	60th AW	*Gold Rusher*
63-8078	1707th ATW	*Spirit of Oklahoma City*
63-8079	437th MAW	*City of Charleston* (second a/c to carry the name)
63-8080	TN ANG	*Night Train to Memphis*
63-8085	63rd MAW	*Spirit of the Inland Empire*
63-8088	1501st ATW	*The Golden Bear*
64-0610	437th MAW	*City of Charleston II South Carolina*

437th MAW C-141B 64-0610 with the nose inscription "Spirit of Charleston South Carolina II," taxiing at Mildenhall in October 1985. (Bob Archer)

Serial	Unit	Name
64-0624	437th MAW	*City of Charleston*
64-0625	436th MAW	*First State Airlifter*
64-0630	437th AW	*Spirit of TSgt Paul E Yonkie*
65-0216	459th AW	*Led by Love of Country*
65-0222	TN ANG	*Draggin' Wagon*
65-0233	60th AW	*City of Suisun*
65-0239	60th AW	*Forty Niners*
65-0257	452nd AMW	*Spirit of the Inland Empire*
65-0259	60th MAW	*City of Fairfield*
65-0265	60th MAW	*City of Sacramento*
65-0267	62nd AW	*Goodbye McChord* (starboard), *Hello Sunshine* (port)

Above: The final 62nd AW Starlifter for retirement, 65-0267, arrived at AMARC for storage on April 9, 2002. The aircraft was suitably inscribed "Good Bye McChord." (Doug Slowiak)

Left: Close-up of retirement markings on the starboard side of 65-0267. (Bob Shane)

"Hello Sunshine" is seen on the nose of 62nd AW C-141B 65-0267. (Phil Kovaric)

Serial	Unit	Name
65-0271	459th AW	*Led by Love of Country*
65-0277	62nd MAW	*Tacoma StarLifter*
65-9410	62nd MAW	*Tacoma StarLifter*
66-0128	63rd MAW	*Spirit of Norton*
66-0137	62nd AW	*City of Tacoma*
66-0139	TN ANG	*Beale Street Blues*
66-0149	436th MAW	*The Peach State*
66-0156	62nd MAW	*Tacoma StarLifter*
66-0157	TN ANG	*Tennessee Pride*
66-0159	62nd AW	*Spirit of the Enlisted Force*
66-0176	63rd MAW	*Inland Empire*

During June 1998, 63rd MAW C-141B 66-0177 was named *Spirit of San Bernardino*. Subsequently, it was earmarked for preservation because of its milestone participation in Operation *Homecoming*. (PMC)

Serial	Unit	Name
66-0177	63rd MAW	*City of San Bernardino*
66-0177	445th AW	*First C-141 to Hanoi*
66-0178	63rd MAW	*Inland Empire*
66-0199	438th MAW	not named, but a Bob Hope cartoon
66-0205	97th AMW	*City of Altus*
66-0206	62nd AW	*Spirit of the Northwest*
66-0207	438th AW	*Spirit of McGuire*
66-7944	62nd MAW	*Tacoma StarLifter*
66-7954	445th AW	*The Mule*
66-7947	438th MAW	*The Garden State Starlifter*
67-0002	437th MAW	*City of Charleston South Carolina*
67-0019	438th MAW	*The Garden State*
67-0021	TN ANG	*Memphis Queen*
67-0024	TN ANG	*Memphis Belle 5*

Short lived inscriptions and artwork have graced the noses and forward fuselages of other Starlifters, especially those whose crews enjoyed success at the various Rodeo competitions.

Tennessee ANG C-141C 67-0024, named *Memphis Belle 5*, taxiing at Fairford in July 1998. (Bob Archer)

Above left: 438th MAW C-141B 67-0019, named *The Garden State*, at McGuire AFB in June 1981 (Bob Stewart)

Above right: Named *City of Charleston South Carolina*, C-141B 67-0002 is seen in February 1969. (Mick Roth)

Above: One of three bicentennial Starlifters, seen on the runway at Frankfurt's Rhein Main AB, 65-0276 was still displaying the special markings in March 1977. (M.Vogel)

Right: Close-up of the nose hexagon of 65-0276 during May 1976. The three bicentennials all had the last two numerals of the serial appropriately ending in "76." (PMC)

The 438th MAW at McGuire AFB applied the bicentennial scheme to the serial of C-141A 63-8076. (Dave Ostrowski)

Above: The 63rd MAW at Norton AFB decorated the tail as well as applying bicentennial markings. C-141A 66-0176 is seen during December 1976. (PMC)

Left: The flamboyant tail scheme on 66-0176 during December 1976. (PMC)

Bicentennial C-141A 66-0176 at Andrews AFB in July 1976. (via EMCS)

Airlift Rodeo/Volant Rodeo

In an attempt to improve the accuracy of aerial delivery, MATS organized the first Computed Air Release Point (CARP) competitions in 1962, with further contests in 1963 and 1964, before the Vietnam War requirements halted the event. It was revived under MAC as the Combat Airlift competition in 1969, when the C-141 participated for the first time, with the 63rd MAW sweeping the

Several Volant Rodeo competitions were hosted at Pope AFB, thanks to large parking areas for visiting aircraft, and the adjacent range at Fort Bragg. Three C-141As and six Bs are seen alongside various US and overseas C-130s, and a lone Fairchild C-123 Provider. (USAF)

Above left: 445th AW C-141C 65-0261, post Volant Rodeo, spells out the disappointment of the crew at not winning the event in July 1998. Graffiti includes a hastily applied face, shark's mouth, and name "War Pig." (Don Spering)

Above right: Another aircraft with Rodeo graffiti, 67-0009 celebrates the "#1 aircrew and team chief" in 1984. (PMC)

board. It was staged again between 1970 and 1972 at various Starlifter bases, before another hiatus due to budgetary issues. The competition was revived yet again in July 1979 as Volant Rodeo and held at Pope AFB, North Carolina, to enable the event to include a wider range of airlifters, including many C-130 units. It was retitled Airlift Rodeo from 1987. Having added the C-130, the competitions were divided into different categories. In 1992, the event was renamed Air Mobility Rodeo, which continued until 2011. However, the Air Force decided that no further Rodeos would take place, as this and other similar competitive flying activities, were not cost effective.

The 514th MAW decorated C-141A 65-9411 following participation in Airlift Rodeo in 1981. The large "#1" clearly indicates they won a category at the event. (Rob Maynard)

Nevertheless, those that did take place were very competitive, with teams chosen from the best of the best to represent each flying unit. Categories involved aircraft preparation, aerial delivery, as well as a maintenance element, plus other related components, with participation by a single aircraft from each operational Wing. Senior MAC personnel noted that the competitive nature had increased the accuracy of airdrops throughout the event, which then permeated throughout squadrons during routine day to day operations.

Nose markings on 65-9411, decorated at the 1981 Airlift Rodeo. (Rob Maynard)

Port side nose of 437th MAW C-141B 65-9401 wearing many additional inscriptions, and the obligatory face around the radome, following success in the 1992 Rodeo. (via EMCS)

Starboard side of 65-9401 during the 1992 event. (via EMCS)

The C-141 continued through until the latter stages of service, with the 63rd MAW being the last Starlifter unit to win the competition outright in 1990. Other C-141 teams also fared well within various categories. Understandably, aircraft were briefly decorated by the winning teams, with chalk or speed tape being improvised to highlight the celebrations. Successful teams occasionally applied a face or shark's mouth, as well as names of participating crews, and messages to denote their prowess. Such graffiti was short lived and was washed off soon afterwards. Interestingly, the 62nd MAW C-141 crew of 65-0258 airdropped a heavy load over a range during Volant Rodeo 1982. The cargo scored a direct hit on a jeep that had been abandoned on the range! The aircraft returned home suitably inscribed as "MAC Bomber" and "62nd Bomb Wing"!

Left: **62nd MAW 65-0258 inscribed "MAC Bomber" at McChord AFB in June 1982 after the aircraft participated in Airlift Rodeo. The crew managed to extract a load during the competition, which scored a direct hit on a parked jeep! (Doug Remington)**

Below: **305th AMW C-141 65-9405 participated in Volant Rodeo in September 1994, crewed by 514th AW personnel, who won one category, and scored in other sections. The aircraft was suitably inscribed to denote their success. (Don Spering)**

Above left: Modestly displaying first place at Volant Rodeo in 1984, 63rd MAW C-141B 66-0179 is at Norton AFB. (PMC)

Above right: Stenciled artwork on C-141B 66-0179 after the 1984 Volant Rodeo. (PMC)

Right: 437th MAW C-141B 64-0618, with the nose number modified to read "4 SICK 18." Despite the derogatory graffiti, the crew did win silverware, with the trophy being proudly displayed. (USAF)

The chalk graffiti notifies the world that the 63rd MAW were judged 1st overall in the 1990 event staged at Little Rock AFB, Arkansas. C-141B 66-0184 is decorated with shark's mouth applied to the nose – interestingly, the chalk adornment would not be so effective on any other color except the European One. (Mike Plonski)

Chapter 6

Ground Trainers

The Sheppard Technical Training Center at Sheppard AFB, Texas, obtained four Starlifters to train personnel on the intricacies of aircraft maintenance. While classroom and computer-based education could prepare prospective technicians with the intricacies of aircraft systems, the opportunity to receive hands-on training could not be fully replicated electronically.

Towards the end of their operational careers, the C-141Bs began to be retired to the Center for a new career as a ground training airframe. The first to be delivered were 66-0176 ex-62nd AW on March 9, 1993, and 66-0126 ex-438th AW on April 6, 1993. They were joined by 65-0228 on April 18, 1994, and 66-0189 the following day, both ex-97th AMW. These were all unofficially designated as GC-141B. With no dedicated crew chief to provide tender loving care on a regular basis, and arrange for exterior cleaning, the Starlifters soon showed signs of oil leaks, which stained several areas, especially the tail. 65-0228 and 66-0189 were only short-term residents, as they were dumped by June 1999, and scrapped by August 2000. The remaining pair fared better, but followed a similar fate, being scrapped during October 2007.

Above: GC-141B 66-0126 is at Sheppard AFB, assigned to the Technical Training Center in April 2001. Note the oil leaks on the tail. (Bob Archer)

Left: C-141B 64-0642 at Altus AFB in April 1984, having been retired and converted to become a static classroom. (Gary James)

Another pair were retired at Altus AFB, Oklahoma, on March 20, 1996, having had the wings and tail assembly removed, in preparation for the technical training role. 64-0642 and 66-0154 were located within a compound and connected to a small building. Both were painted mid gray with no other markings. 64-0642 was subsequently transferred to Quartz Mountain Regional Airport at Altus for ground instruction training.

At Travis AFB, C-141B 65-0246 was retired for a similar task as the pair at Altus. The aircraft was damaged by fire in a taxiing accident at Travis on April 15, 1986, when the right wing struck a light pole. The aircraft donated the left wing to 67-0029 when that aircraft sustained damage. 65-0246 was painted mid gray overall, with "ground trainer" on the nose. The airframe was subsequently struck off change on June 15, 2001, and presumably scrapped.

A number of others were retired, including 64-0644 at McGuire AFB for battle damage repair training by September 2000; 64-0653 at Brooks AFB, Texas, on April 15, 2007; 65-0233 at Laguna Army Airfield, Arizona, on July 29, 1993; and 65-0236 and 66-0161, both ground instructional airframes, at Scott AFB on September 8, 1993, and at Kelly Field, Joint Base San Antonio, Texas, on February 4, 2003, respectively.

Right: C-141B 65-0246 suffered the port side wing being destroyed by fire off during a taxiing accident at Travis AFB on October 15, 1986. The fuselage was subsequently employed for instructional training before being scrapped. (PMC)

Below: After spending six months withdrawn from use at Mildenhall, and being partially cannibalized, 60th AMW C-141B 65-0268 performed a brief air test, before returning to Travis AFB on April 12, 1997. (Phil Cossey)

Former 305th AMW C-141B 66-0160 at Eglin AFB during September 2003, being evaluated for simulated nerve agent contamination tests. The Starlifter was sprayed with tripropyl phosphate ahead of being cleaned to a safe level. (AFHRA)

60th AMW C-141B 65-0268 arrived at Mildenhall, UK, on October 27, 1996 and appeared to take up residence. The aircraft remained parked and occasionally donated components to other Starlifters requiring repair. However, unexpectedly, the aircraft performed an air test on April 11, 1997, before departing the following day for Travis AFB. It was seen there on April 19, two days before making its final flight to Davis-Monthan AFB for storage. It is believed the Starlifter suffered a technical problem at Mildenhall, which was not a priority to repair, due to the impending retirement.

Between September 8 and 24, 2003, former 305th AMW C-141B 66-0160 was at Eglin AFB, Florida, for a unique experiment. The aircraft was the subject of a test to discover solutions to aircraft contaminated by chemical and biological agents. The test was staged by the Defense Threat Reduction Agency and was designed to decontaminate a large aircraft and return to service. To contaminate, the C-141 was sprayed with tripropyl phosphate to simulate weapons-grade chemical nerve agent VX. All windows and doors were sealed, with the aircraft covered with suction-powered collection funnels to measure the contaminated liquid and vapor. The cleaning process was monitored extremely closely to ensure the contaminated areas were unpolluted to better than that deemed to be the minimum safe level. The 46th Test Wing provided the tarmac area and administered the test. Following completion of the evaluation, the aircraft was retired to Davis-Monthan AFB, arriving on October 1, 2003.

Retirement

The Starlifter was retired over a protracted period, with the first C-141B, 66-0143 of the 97th AMW, arriving for storage and reclamation with AMARC at Davis-Monthan AFB, Arizona, on May 11, 1993. The last two active-duty C-141Bs in operational service were 64-0633 and 67-0012 with the 305th AMW, which were both flown for storage on September 16, 2004.

Having had a cockpit upgrade, the C-141C version remained in service slightly longer. 64-0632 of the Mississippi ANG was the first C to be retired, beginning storage on December 3, 2002. The honor of operating the final C-141s befell the 445th AW at Wright-Patterson. Their penultimate aircraft was C-141C 64-0620, which left the base for storage on January 12, 2006. Suitably handwritten on the nose in felt tip pen was the inscription "The Last C-141 Delivered to the Boneyard" and "So Long Starlifter."

Above: NC-141A 61-2777 is in storage with AMARC at Davis-Monthan AFB in November 1994. (Chris Lofting)

Right: The end of the line for NC-141A 61-2777 and C-141B 65-0268, as they await removal to the HVF West yard outside Davis-Monthan AFB in February 2004. (Bob Shane)

Above: The second C-141 to be retired was 63rd AW 65-9398, parked here at AMARC in December 1993, five months after arriving. (PMC)

Right: Seven of the first batch of C-141Bs to be retired, headed by 66-0143, 65-9398, 64-0636, and 64-0648, seen here at AMARC in December 1993. (PMC)

The flight's final aircrew all had their names written beneath the inscription, along with the message "It's Been Fun." Few associated with the Starlifter would disagree!

However, the final Starlifter in service was C-141C 66-0177, which was the *Hanoi Taxi*. The aircraft was retired to the National Museum of the US Air Force at Wright-Patterson. The significance of the aircraft in repatriating former POWs from Hanoi was such that the Air Force elected to commemorate the retirement with a large ceremony on May 6, 2006, attended by many POWs. A final flight above the assembled personnel took place before official transfer to the museum.

A total of 238 entered AMARC, consisting of 163 C-141Bs, 12 C-141B SOLL IIs, 61 C-141Cs, and two NC-141As. The majority were cannibalized for their engines and other components, before being

Above: Four C-141Bs, retired between December 1997 and July 1998, show signs of paint scheme deterioration in the desert climate. Serials 67-0009, 66-0200, 65-0272 and 66-0135 are seen during April 2001. (Bob Archer)

Left: A row of C-141Cs in storage with AMARC, including 64-0620, which was the 238th and last to be sent for storage, arriving on January 12, 2006. (Karl Drage)

Soon after arrival for storage at AMARC, Mississippi ANG C-141C 64-0632 is seen with inventory identity number "AACR0168" applied. Additionally, the crew chief, TSgt P Patterson, has inscribed the fuel remaining, the arrival date of "3 Dec 2002," and that the auxiliary power unit is ineffective! (Woodie Hall)

Above: The first ten Starlifters to be retired to AMARC did so beginning in May 1993, initiated by 66-0143, 65-9398, and 65-9410. By October 1995, these early arrivals had donated many parts to enable other C-141s to remain operational, as can be seen by the remnants on the desert floor. NC-141A 61-2777 was a later arrival, parked for convenience. (Bob Archer)

Right: Nose markings of C-141C 65-0271 of 459th AW soon after arrival at AMARC on September 2, 2003. (Doug Slowiak)

cut up into sections and sold for scrap. Most, if not all, were sold to HVF West, which operate a large yard situated outside of AMARC. The sectioned aircraft were either loaded aboard flatbed trucks for the short journey or towed behind a tractor unit. Once at HVF West's premises, the components were quickly shredded, and were smelted into ingots for recycling.

Never a Dull Moment for a Starlifter Crew

The C-141 was at the heart of the Inter-Continental Ballistic Missile nuclear deterrence mission. The Boeing LGM-30 Minuteman ICBM final assembly facility was at Air Force Planet 77 in Ogden, Utah, with transport aircraft flying into nearby Hill AFB, to collect from and deliver to air bases adjacent to the missile silos across the Midwestern US. C-141A 64-0609 was accepted by the USAF in April

64-0609 was delivered to the Air Force on April 16, 1965, and briefly joined the ASD to evaluate loading techniques and delivery of Boeing LGM-30 Minuteman ICBMs. The need was to ferry fully assembled missiles from Ogden, Utah, to the nearest military air base in the vicinity of launch silos in the US Midwest. (Richard Sullivan)

1965 and was with the ASD at Wright-Patterson AFB one month later. The aircraft evaluated the transportation of a complete Minuteman missile ahead of the mission being allocated to the Starlifter. Having proved that the Starlifter was capable of the mission, the C-141 became a fairly frequent visitor to SAC bases. Each Strategic Missile Wing was located at an Air Force Base with the infrastructure sufficient to handle a C-141 and its single ICBM cargo. Missiles were delivered to and from their dispersed silos inside special Transporter Erector Loader (TEL) trailers. However, the TELs were too large to be accommodated inside a C-141, requiring the missile to be unpacked.

C-141 in Combat
During the Tet Offensive in January 1968, 4th MAS loadmaster Jeff Larsen reported that his crew were alerted to fly from Clark AB to Tan Son Nhut AB, South Vietnam, which was closed at the time due to insurgent activity. The mission was to offload ten pallets, and evacuate the passenger terminal, which included the Assistant Secretary of the Navy. The sortie required exceptional crew skills, as Saigon was under siege. Due to the insurgents shooting at the Starlifter, the crew aborted the first landing. The second landing was successful, with the rapid offload/loading carried out with all four engines running. A maximum-performance takeoff preceded a flight to Taiwan, and safety. The crew were later advised that this was the first recognized combat operation by a C-141.

Hijack Attempt

During the lifetime of the Starlifter, there were at least two attempted hijackings of the type. Sometime prior to November 1970, C-141A 66-0192 was awaiting cargo while at Bien Hoa AB, South Vietnam. The six crew members were relaxing in the cargo hold, while the aircraft commander was at the command post. A young US Army private, carrying an M-16 rifle, entered through the open ramp, and ordered the crew into the cockpit and demanded they fly him "somewhere."

Having started the engines and attempted to taxi, security vehicles blocked their path. The hijacker ordered the loadmaster into the cargo compartment, then shot him three times. The crew radioed that the loadmaster had been shot. The vehicles cleared the taxiway, but, for a second time, blocked the aircraft's path. Throughout this tense encounter, the crew were able to communicate over headsets without the hijacker's knowledge.

At a prearranged time, the navigator grabbed the rifle barrel while the copilot and engineer tackled the hijacker. During the struggle, 13 rounds were fired into the cockpit. The crew members were able to overpower and disarm the hijacker before handing him over to the security police. The injured loadmaster was taken to hospital by a Kaman HH-43 Husky, where he received treatment from which he survived. He was subsequently medically discharged. Maintenance personnel made temporary repairs to the aircraft before the jet was returned home. Details of the second attempted hijack are not known.

Unusual Cargo 1

The cargo carried by C-141 crews was not always the most essential, seemingly. Ships brought thousands of cartons of cigarettes to the port at Subic Bay, Philippines, for the vast numbers of Americans in the region. Once unloaded, some were taken by truck to the base exchange at Clark Air Base, a journey of 50 miles. However, the trucks were hijacked so frequently that an alternative delivery method had to be found. The solution was to arrange for the cargo of cigarettes to be driven the short distance to Naval Air Station Cubi Point then flown by C-141 to Clark. As one pilot remarked, the distance of just 50 miles was so short that he barely had time to retract the undercarriage!

Unusual Cargo 2

Medical related missions rapidly became a regular feature for the Starlifter, primarily due to the speed of the aircraft. The urgent need for blood transfusions for wounded personnel in SEA required regular shipments from the US. Organized by the Whole Blood Processing Laboratory at McGuire AFB, shipments were flown to a blood bank in Japan. From there, they were forwarded to Vietnam. With a shelf life of just three weeks, and temperature control critical, the C-141 had to be flown smoothly, as turbulence could separate the blood consistency rendering it unusable.

Chapter 7

Operating Units

The C-141 was flown by a single service (MATS) and several commands within the active duty, as well as the Air Force Reserve and Air National Guard. The unit designations and titles changed periodically throughout the 42 years of Starlifter assignment. The majority of units were devoted to airlift, although a small number performed other tasks. The details that follow are the month and year when each squadron operated the C-141. In several instances, squadrons were transitioning from the C-141 to more modern equipment, such as the C-17A, with both types operational for a time.

Above left: Seven 63rd MAW C-141Bs on the flight line at Norton AFB in June 1982. The nearest is 66-0128, with the inscription "Spirit of Norton" on the nose. (PMC)

Above right: Close-up of "Spirit of Norton" on the nose of 66-0128. (PMC)

Left: Former 97th AMW C-141B 66-0206 during the final stages of destruction at Davis-Monthan AFB on October 19, 2005. A CAT digger is seen slicing through the fuselage before carting the residue to the HVF yard outside the base. (Doug Slowiak)

The dates presented for the commands are when the particular organization was formed, which, in most cases, was either before or after Starlifter service. The corresponding dates for Wings, Groups, and Squadrons are those when the C-141 was operated, and not necessarily when the relevant unit was formed or inactivated. The commands are presented alphabetically, and with the reserves at the end, whereas the Wings, Groups and Squadrons are numerical and self-explanatory.

Air Education & Training Command (July 1, 1992–Current)
97th Air Mobility Wing – Altus AFB, October 1992–August 2001
57th Airlift Squadron, October 1992–August 2001

The 97th AMW was activated at Altus AFB on October 1, 1992, to replace the 443rd MAW. The Wing was assigned to AETC, performing aircrew training for the C-5 Galaxy and KC-135R, as well as the C-141. The Starlifter was assigned until 2001, when C-141 training was reassigned to the 445th MAW at Wright-Patterson AFB under AFRC.

C-141B 65-0276 at Robins AFB in June 1992, having had the wing box replaced, and awaiting the wings to be refitted. (Frank J Mirande)

Air Force Logistics Command (April 1, 1961–July 1, 1992)
Warner Robins Air Logistics Center – Robins AFB, January 1966–July 1992
2875th Test Squadron, January 1988–July 1992

The Warner Robins Air Logistics Center was the sole USAF major overhaul facility for the C-141, although the manufacturer and other civilian contractors also performed modifications and upgrades. The ALC had a small cadre of test pilots who carried out post-maintenance flights prior to the aircraft being returned to operational service. The Center did not have a numerical unit assigned until 1988 when a Test Squadron was established.

Retired C-141C 65-0248 making its final journey during April 2005 from Robins AFB to the base Museum of Aviation. (Dave Webb)

Air Force Materiel Command (July 1, 1992–Current)
412th Test Wing – Edwards AFB, May 1993–August 1998
418th Test Squadron, May 1993–March 1994
418th Flight Test Squadron, March 1994–August 1998
    Formed as the 412th Test Wing at Edwards AFB, on October 2, 1992, it replaced the 6510th Test Wing. The four NC-141As were assigned when transferred from Wright-Patterson AFB, joining the 418th Test Squadron, which was also formed on October 2. It was redesignated 418th Flight Test Squadron on March 1, 1994. The final NC-141A was retired in 1998. It very briefly evaluated the C-141C ahead of the version entering service.

4950th Test Wing – Wright-Patterson AFB, July 1992–May 1993
4953rd Test Squadron, July 1992–May 1993
    See under AFSC for more details.

Warner Robins Air Logistics Center – Robins AFB, July 1992–March 2005
2875th Test Squadron, July–October 1992
339th Test Squadron, October 1992–March 1994
339th Flight Test Squadron, March 1994–March 2005
    The Warner Robins ALC became part of the Air Force Materiel Command when the new organization replaced both the Air Force Logistics Command and Air Force Systems Command. No changes were made to the working practices, as this was just a merger of two previously separate organizations into one.

One of only two test Starlifters operated in a non-standard external color scheme, NC-141A 61-2777 of the ASD at Wright-Patterson AFB is seen in September 1970. It was extensively modified for development of the Rockwell B-1 tail warning system, amongst other related tasks. (Tom Brewer)

Air Force Systems Command (February 1, 1950–July 1, 1992)

Aeronautical Systems Division – Wright-Patterson AFB, April 1967–March 1971
4950th Test Wing – Wright-Patterson AFB, March 1971–July 1992
4953rd Test Squadron, July 1975–July 1992

The Wing was activated at Wright-Patterson on March 1, 1971, gaining the four NC/C-141As already in residence. Prior to the unit being formed, the Starlifters and other aircraft were directly assigned to the ASD. The Division was also involved in the evaluation of the C-141 ahead of the type being introduced into service. At the completion of this phase, ASD retained four Starlifters to be used for a variety of test programs. The 4950th TW was absorbed into AFMC in July 1992, prior to inactivating in June 1994. The majority of aircraft had by that time relocated to Edwards AFB, including the NC-141As.

4950th Test Wing (TW) NC-141A 61-2777 at Davis-Monthan AFB in January 1983, with extensive modifications to support the Rockwell B-1B program. (Paul Bennett)

Air Force Flight Test Center – Edwards AFB, June 25, 1951–July 6, 2012
    Various numbered units were formed as subordinate to the AAFTC. Activated in 1951 to evaluate every new and extensively modified aircraft type, the AFFTC was assigned eight C-141As initially, to ensure that the new airlifter was capable of fully functioning as required. These were assigned from the very beginning of Starlifter operations, with four transferred to MATS, while the other four were relocated to ASD. Subsequently, when ASD ceased operations, the four aircraft returned to the AFFTC circa May 1993. The last NC-141A retired in August 1998 – see the 412th Test Wing under AFMC. The AFFTC also became a component of AFMC on July 1, 1992, but is detailed here only, to avoid duplication.

Military Air Transport Service (June 1, 1948–January 1, 1966)
1501st Air Transport Wing – Travis AFB, April 1965–January 1966
44th Air Transport Squadron, April 1965–January 1966
75th ATS, November 1965–January 1966
    The Wing had already been established at Travis AFB for 17 years when the first C-141As were delivered. The 1501st initiated Starlifter operations before inactivating when replaced by the 60th MAW on January 8, 1966.

1607th ATW – Dover AFB, August 1965–January 1966
20th ATS, August 1965–January 1966
    As with other four-digit designated units, the 1607th was already active at Dover AFB when the C-141A began to arrive in August 1965. The 1607th was replaced by the 436th MAW on January 8, 1966.

1608th ATW – Charleston AFB, August 1965–January 1966
3rd ATS, August 1965–January 1966
    The 1608th at Charleston AFB had nine C-141As delivered by January 8, 1966, when the unit was replaced by the 437th MAW.

1611th ATW – McGuire AFB, January 1966
No C-141 service
    The 1611th was planned to receive the C-141A, but was inactivated on January 8, 1966, prior to the initial deliveries. It was replaced by the 438th MAW at McGuire AFB.

1707th ATW – Tinker AFB, October 1964–January 1966
1741st ATS, October 1964–January 1966
    The 1707th accepted the first operational C-141A in October 1964. The training unit was only a short-term operator, as the unit inactivated on January 8, 1966, when replaced by the 443rd MAW.

Named *Gold Rusher*, 60th AW C-141B 63-8075 is seen at Kadena AB during March 1993. (Alan Winzerling)

66-0191 is seen at Mildenhall in September 1995, with the final black and white tail stripe design of the 60th AMW applied to Travis Starlifters. (Bob Archer)

Military Airlift Command (January 1, 1966–June 1, 1992)/Air Mobility Command (June 1, 1992–Current)

60th MAW/AW/AMW – Travis AFB, January 1966–December 1997

7th MAS/AS, March 1971–October 1993 – to McChord AFB

19th AS, October 1993–July 1996

20th AS, October 1993–November 1997

44th MAS, January 1966–March 1972

75th MAS, January 1966–October 1970

86th MAS/AS, April 1966–October 1993

The 60th MAW was formed on January 8, 1966, replacing the 1501st ATW, when the majority of four-digit units were realigned. The new Wing gained the 28 C-141As that had been delivered to the 44th and 75th ATSs – which were then redesignated as MASs.

The location of the air base, to the northeast of San Francisco, was ideal as one of the primary airlift hubs linking the United States with the air bases in SEA. South Vietnam, in particular, was often the destination of C-141s departing Travis, although other bases in SEA and the western Pacific region in general were also the final stop for Starlifter crews. Furthermore, Travis was also the primary air base for wounded personnel from the Vietnam theater being repatriated home.

Interestingly, the first C-141A to be delivered to an operational unit was at Travis AFB. The 1501st ATW officially accepted 63-8088 into service on April 23, 1965, with transfer to the 60th nine months later. The aircraft remained stationed at Travis AFB until retired on March 17, 1996 and was, therefore, unique in being assigned to just one location throughout its 31-year career. Total flying hours were 41,470, which included many sorties to Vietnam. After languishing on the main ramp at Travis, the aircraft was overhauled by volunteers, before being dedicated for display on September 16, 2005. Despite the Heritage Center at the base proudly stating that 63-8088 repatriated 591 POWs from the Vietnam War in 1973, this was clearly not the case, as the details presented within the chapter on Operation *Homecoming* do not list this aircraft.

62nd MAW C-141B 65-0241 taxiing in July 1985 at McChord AFB. (Carl E Porter)

62d MAW/AW – McChord AFB, August 1966–June 2002
4th MAS/AS, April 1970–April 2000
7th AS, October 1993–July 1999
8th MAS/AS, August 1966–June 2002
36th MAS/AS, October 1989–October 1993

The 62nd ATW became an MAW on January 8, 1966, when it transferred from MATS to MAC. The first C-141A was not assigned until August 1966, with the Wing operating the new Starlifter alongside the Douglas C-124 Globemaster. The 4th MAS transitioned in 1970, increasing the number of Starlifters and enabling the C-124s to join the reserves.

During the C-124 era, the Wing was tasked with delivering the warheads, and other components of "special weapons" from the arsenals in the US to the NATO bases in Europe. When the C-141 began deliveries, the Wing retained this task.

63rd MAW C-141B 66-0150 in Australia during October 1987 supporting the Thunderbirds display team. (PMC)

Above: The prestige associated with supporting the Air Force's national team required the C-141 to have an immaculate appearance. 66-0150 was probably fresh from a major overhaul and repaint at the Warner Robins ALC to ensure no maintenance issues. (PMC)

Right: Occupying the foremost position on the tail, the Thunderbirds emblem is centrally placed, demoting the Wing badge to a lower position. (PMC)

63rd MAW/AW – Norton AFB, April 1967–September 1993
14th MAS/AS, April 1967–April 1992
15th MAS/AS, April 1967–July 1993
52nd MAS/AS, June 1988–September 1992
53rd MAS/AS, January 1972–April 1993

The 63rd Military Airlift Wing (Provisional) was formed at Norton AFB on July 1, 1966, while the parent unit, the 63rd MAW, was in residence at Hunter AFB. The Provisional status was created to enable the unit at Norton AFB to re-equip with the C-141A, while the parent unit gradually ran down C-124 operations at Hunter AFB. The 63rd MAW moved to Norton on April 1, 1967, assuming the mission, personnel, and aircraft of the Provisional unit, which was discontinued. Only two aircraft were delivered prior to the Wing officially moving to Norton, with a further ten arriving during the next five weeks.

Due to the proximity of Norton AFB to Vandenberg AFB (both in the vicinity of Los Angeles), the 63rd was tasked with ferrying Minuteman ICBMs from the Boeing plant in Ogden, Utah, as well as the SAC missile base to the latter facility for various reasons.

The 63rd was the last MAC unit to re-equip, and the first under AMC to relinquish the Starlifter. Despite the Wing inactivating, the Norton-based squadrons were reassigned to other units, with their heritage retained.

305th AMW SOLL II 64-0630 taxiing at Mildenhall in September 2000. Unlike the white scheme, which did not show dirt and stains, and European One, which was too dark to see such marks, the AMC Proud Gray enhanced grime. (Bob Archer)

305th AMW – McGuire AFB, October 1994–September 2004

6th AS, October 1994–September 2004

13th AS, October 1994–March 2000

18th AS, October 1994–July 1995

The 305th Air Mobility Wing relocated from Grissom AFB, Indiana, to McGuire AFB, New Jersey, on October 1, 1994 to assume the assets of the 438th MAW. AMW status was assigned as the unit operated the McDonnell Douglas KC-10A Extender, as well as the C-141B. The Starlifter was assigned until 2004, when it was replaced by the C-17A.

C-141B 64-0633 of the 305th AMW departing McGuire AFB for the last time for the flight to David-Monthan AFB and storage. In company with 67-0012, the two Starlifters left on September 16, 2004, thereby ending C-141 operations at the base. (USAF)

Above left: 305th AMW C-141B 64-0633, with flags protruding out of the roof, during the retirement ceremony at McGuire AFB. (USAF)

Above right: After arrival at Davis-Monthan AFB, crew members signed the forward fuselage of their aircraft. The retirement of the Starlifter was very poignant for both air and ground crews. (Woodie Hall)

436th MAW – Dover AFB, January 1966–August 1973
9th MAS, January 1966–September 1968
20th MAS, January 1966–August 1973
58th MAS at Robins AFB, January 1967–August 1971

Activated on January 8, 1966, at Dover AFB to replace the 160th ATW, it inherited the C-124s, C-133s, and the C-141s of that unit. It operated the C-141A until 1973, when the unit switched to the C-5A Galaxy. The Wing was responsible for the geographically separated 58th MAS, which flew the Starlifter at Robins AFB from January 15, 1966 to August 15, 1971.

436th MAW C-141A 66-0166 at Pearce AB, Australia, in May 1966, just three months after delivery on February 20. Note the unit designation presented on the main wheel well with a black and white diagonal background. This marking was removed not long afterwards. (Ben Dannecker)

437th AW C-141B 67-0002 during a visit to Rhein Main AB during December 1995, while supporting USAF operations in the Balkans. (Joop de Groot)

437th MAW/AW – Charleston AFB, January 1966–June 2000
3rd MAS, January 1966–June 1970
14th AS, April 1992–February 1995
15th AS, October 1993–June 1997
16th AS, October 1993–June 2000
17th MAS/AS, August 1987–June 1993
20th MAS/AS, August 1973–October 1993
41st MAS, February 1967–April 1992
76th MAS/AS, January 1966–October 1993

   The 437th MAW began C-141 operations when formed on January 8, 1966, to replace the 1608th ATW. It flew the Starlifter officially until June 15, 2000. Interestingly, the 14th AS achieved the remarkable safety record on March 25, 1997, when the unit completed 750,000 flight hours, over a period of 50 years, without an accident – flying the C-124C, C-141A/B, and the new C-17A.

438th AW 66-0155 named *Jersey Express* in November 1992. (Paolo Rollino)

A trio of natural metal finish C-141As of the 438th MAW at McGuire AFB in August 1980. (Steve Williams)

438th MAW/AW – McGuire AFB, August 1967–October 1994
6th MAS/AS, April 1970–October 1994
13th AS, October 1993–October 1994
18th MAS/AS, August 1968–October 1994
30th MAS/AS, August 1967–October 1993

The Wing was formed on January 8, 1966, to replace the 1611th ATW, although the latter was not a Starlifter unit, as the first example was not delivered until August 1967. It operated the C-141 until inactivated on October 1, 1994, when it was replaced by the 305th AMW.

The final Starlifter built, 67-0166 was operated by the 443rd MAW on behalf of Commander-in-Chief of Military Airlift Command. Finished in an attractive white upper surface, with a gold cheatline, and white overall engine nacelles, it is seen here in July 1994. (PMC)

443d MAW – Tinker AFB/Altus AFB, January 1966–October 1992

57th MAS, January 1966–October 1992

Formed on January 8, 1966, at Tinker AFB to replace the 1707th ATW, it inherited their assets and personnel for the training role. The Wing relocated to Altus AFB on May 5, 1969. It was inactivated on October 1, 1992, when it was replaced by the 97th AMW. The Wing operated the C-141 throughout its 26 years of operations.

C-141B 66-0189 was recently reassigned to the 443rd MAW in March 1988 (Lewis Grant)

Air Force Reserve (June 21, 1968–February 17, 1997)/Air Force Reserve Command (February 17, 1997–Current)

315th MAW/AW (Associate) – Charleston AFB, July 1973–June 2000

300th MAS/AS (A), July 1973–October 1994

300th AS, October 1994–June 1997

701st MAS/AS (A), July 1973–October 1994

701st AS, October 1994–October 1997

707th MAS/AS (A), July 1973–October 1994

707th AS, October 1994–June 2000

Activated as the 315th Military Airlift Wing (Associate) on July 1, 1973, to replace the 943rd MAG (A). It was redesignated 315th AW (Associate) on February 1, 1992, before relinquishing the Associate status on October 1, 1994. It retired the Starlifter in 2000.

349th MAW/AW (A) – Travis AFB, July 1973–November 1997

708th MAS/AS (A), July 1973–October 1994

708th AS, October 1994–September 1996

710th MAS/AS (A), July 1973–October 1994

710th AS, October 1994–November 1997

349th MAW (A) formed on July 25, 1969, as the parent organization for the 938th MAG (A). It replaced the latter on January 1, 1972. It was then redesignated 349th AW (A) on February 1, 1992, and 349th AW on October 1, 1994. It retired the C-141 in November 1997.

Above: 445th AW C-141C 66-7954, with artwork and name *The Mule*, at Mildenhall. (Matthew Clements)

Right: Close-up of *The Mule*, with appropriate artwork superimposed over a map of Ohio. (Phil Kovaric)

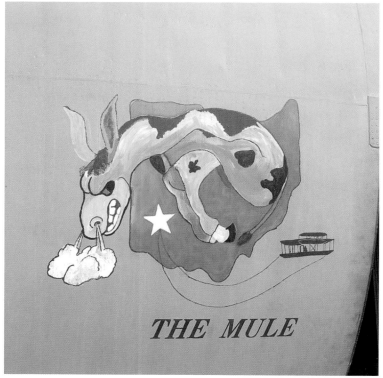

THE MULE

445th MAW/AW (A) – Norton AFB, July 1973–July 1993, and March AFB, July 1993–May 1994

728th MAS (A), July 1973–January 1992

729th MAS (A), July 1973–February 1992

729th AS (A), February 1992–April 1993

729th AS, April 1993–May 1994

730th MAS (A), July 1973–February 1992

730th AS (A), February 1992–April 1993

730th AS, April 1993–May 1994

445th AW – Wright-Patterson AFB, October 1994–May 2006

89th AS, October 1994–June 2005

356th AS, October 1994–May 2006

Re-formed as the 445th MAW (Associate) on July 1, 1973, at Norton AFB to provide personnel to augment the active duty 63rd MAW. It replaced the 944th MAG (A). It then changed to 445th AW (A) on February 1, 1992, and 445th AW on April 1, 1993. On April 1, 1993, the 445th was the first Associate unit to transition to its own equipment, flying the C-141. It relocated to March AFB on July 1, 1993 but inactivated on May 1, 1994. It returned to operations on October 1, 1994 at Wright-Patterson AFB. It flew the C-141 throughout. The latter period of activation was as the C-141 schoolhouse (training unit), which was performed until May 2006, when the unit retired the Starlifter.

62nd MAW C-141B 66-0159, inscribed with "Spirit of the Enlisted Force," during July 1998. (Don Spering)

446th MAW/AW (A) – McChord AFB, July 1973–June 2002

97th MAS/AS (A), July 1973–October 1994

97th AS, October 1994–April 2000

313th MAS/AS (A), July 1973–October 1994

313th AS, October 1994–July 1999

728th AS, January 1992–June 2002

Redesignated as the 446th MAW (A) on July 1, 1973, it was attached to the co-located 62nd MAW. It replaced the 939th MAG(A). It then changed to 446th AW(A) on February 1, 1992, and 446th AW on October 1, 1994.

452nd AMW C-141 66-7952 is suitably embellished with details of the locations visited during a world tour. It appears the crew enjoyed all the destinations, apart from Cape Verde, West Africa. (Marcel Rodate)

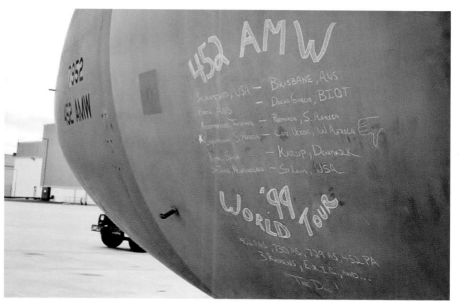

A very happy crew from the 452nd AMW with the silverware after winning the maintenance category at Rodeo 2000. (Marcel Rodate)

452d AMW – March AFB/ARB, May 1994–June 2005
729th AS, May 1994–June 2005
730th AS, May 1994–June 2005
  Redesignated the 452nd AMW on May 1, 1994, the Air Mobility Wing status was applied as the unit flew the KC-135 alongside the C-141. It operated the Starlifter from 1994 until 2005.

459th MAW/AW – Andrews AFB, July 1986–September 2003
756th MAS, July 1986–February 1992
756th AS, February 1992–September 2003
  Formed as the 459th MAW on July 1, 1986 and redesignated 459th AW on August 1, 1992, the unit operated the C-141B and, later, the C-141C between 1986 and 2003, before transitioning to the KC-135R.

514th MAW/AW (A) – McGuire AFB, July 1973–October 1994
514th AMW – McGuire AFB, October 1994–September 2004
335th MAS/AS (A), July 1973–September 1995
702nd MAS/AS (A), July 1973–February 1992
702nd AS (A), February 1992–October 1994
702nd AS, October 1994–March 2000
732nd MAS/AS (A), July 1973–October 1994
732nd AS, October 1994–September 2004
  Re-formed as the 514th MAW(A) on September 25, 1968, to administer the 903rd MAG (A). It then replaced the latter in July 1973. It was attached to the 438th MAW/305th AMW.

903rd MAG (A) – McGuire AFB, April 1970–July 1973
335th MAS (A), April 1970–July 1973
702nd MAS (A), December 1970–July 1973
732d MAS (A), April 1970–July 1973
  Seven Military Airlift Groups within the 900 numerical sequence were Starlifter operators, six of which were Associate units, supporting an active duty wing. In the case of the 903rd, this was supporting the 438th MAW. The Group was only operational until July 1973 when inactivated, having been replaced by the 514th MAW (A). It is worth noting that the unit structure of the reserves was a bewildering arrangement until the early 1970s. None of these six had aircraft directly assigned, and the reservist unit number was not presented on the nose alongside the active duty wing designation.

907th AG – Rickenbacker AFB, February 1992–April 1993; Wright-Patterson AFB April 1993–October 1994
356th AS, February 1992–October 1994
  This was the only 900 series reservist unit that had aircraft directly assigned, albeit only briefly, as the Group was replaced by the 445th AW.

912th MAG (A) – Dover AFB, September 1968–July 1973
326th MAS (A), September 1968–July 1973
  Despite the active duty 436th MAW having three C-141 squadrons, only one Associate squadron was in place. The single reservist unit was responsible for augmenting active duty personnel for all three squadrons of the 436th. The 912th was replaced by the 512th MAW (A), although the new wing switched to the C-5A at the same time, and was not a C-141 operator.

938th MAG (A) – Travis AFB, July 1969–July 1973
301st MAS (A), July 1969–July 1973
312th MAS (A), July 1969–July 1973

In the majority of instances, a reservist Group was in place where there was only one flying squadron in residence. However, the reservist unit structure had several such anomalies, including at Travis, where a single Group was responsible for two Associate squadrons. The Group supported the active duty 60th MAW until July 1973, when it was replaced by the 349th MAW (A).

939th MAG (A) – McChord AFB, July 1968–July 1973
97th MAS (A), July 1969–July 1973
313th MAS (A), July 1968–July 1973

The 939th had two Associate squadrons matching the pair of active-duty MASs of the 62nd MAW. As with other Groups, the 939th was inactivated in July 1973, when replaced by the 446th MAW (A).

943d MAG (A) – Charleston AFB, September 1969–July1973
300th MAS (A), September 1969–July 1973
701st MAS (A), September 1970–July1973
707th MAS (A), October 1972–July 1973

Three Associate squadrons were formed to enable one each to augment personnel with the active-duty squadrons of the 437th MAW. The Group was replaced by the 315th MAW (A).

944th MAG (A) – Norton AFB, March 1968–July 1973
728th MAS (A), January 1972–July 1973
729th MAS (A), April 1969–July 1973
730th MAS (A), March 1968–July 1973

Another AFRes Group administering three Associate squadrons, which was replaced by the 445th MAW (A).

Tennessee ANG C-141C 65-0222, named *Draggin' Wagon*. (Phil Kovaric)

Above left: **Nose art of C-141C 67-0024** *Memphis Belle 5*. **(Phil Kovaric)**

Above right: **61-2778 was named** *Father Time* **and inscribed "Oldest Production C-141." The Tennessee ANG named almost all their Starlifters. (Tennessee ANG)**

Below: *Memphis Queen* **C-141C 67-0021 of the Tennessee ANG. (Guido Latz)**

Air National Guard (September 18, 1947–Current)

164th MAG/AW – Memphis International Airport, Tennessee, March 1992–May 2004
155th MAS/AS, March 1992–May 2004

Surprisingly, only two Air National Guard units flew the C-141. The ANG units had a complement of some eight or nine Starlifters at any given time. Both units maintained their aircraft in the finest tradition of the ANG. Furthermore, both squadrons had their aircraft painted in a gloss gray scheme, which was far more attractive that the matt finish applied by all other users.

The Wing was located at Memphis IAP, the city home to Elvis Presley. Quite naturally, the unit used call sign "Elvis" for many of its sorties. Its last aircraft was 66-0157, which departed on May 2, 2004.